Answers

to

Frequently **A**sked **Q**uestions

on

Parenting

[PART 1]

Drs. Ekram & Mohamed Rida Beshir

amana publications

© 2005AC /1426AH

amana publications
10710 Tucker Street
Beltsville, MD 20705-2223 USA
Tel. 301-595-5777, 800-660-1777
Fax 301-595-5888, 240-250-3000
Email: amana@amana-corp.com
www.amanapublications.com

First Edition
2005AC /1426AH

Reprint
2017AC /1438AH

ISBN 1-59008-036-X / 978-1-59008--036-8 (13-digit)

Library of Congress Cataloging-in-Publication Data

Beshir, Ekram.
 Answers to frequently asked questions on parenting / Ekram Beshir and
M. Rida Beshir.– 1st ed.
    p. cm.
 Includes bibliographical references.
 ISBN 1-59008-036-X (alk. paper)
 1. Child rearing–Religious aspects–Islam. 2. Parenting–Religious
aspects–Islam. 3. Muslim youth–North America–Conduct of life. I.
Beshir, Mohamed Rida. II. Title.

 HQ769.3.B45 2005
 297.5'77–dc22

                                    2005022410

Printed by Mega Printing in Turkey

Acknowledgments

We would like to express our sincere gratitude to our good friend, Jennifer Templin, for all the time and hard work she put into editing this book. We will be forever indebted to her for her gracious support and dedication to this work. May Allah bless her, keep her on the Straight Path and reward her with *jannah*.

We kindly request that every reader make *du'a* for her.

Introduction

A t various conferences and conventions, when conducting parenting workshops and presenting lectures on the subject of raising children in North American society, we usually allocate time to answer questions from the audience. We try our best during these question and answer sessions to respond in the most comprehensive way. However, with a hot topic such as parenting, particularly in North America, there is never enough time to give detailed answers and, at the same time, respond to as many questions as possible. In addition, some of these questions have been raised more than once in recent years. Because of this, we feel that these questions represent crucial issues of concern occupying the minds of a great majority of parents. As such, they deserve to be addressed in enough detail to be clarified and to provide Muslim parents with the proper advice supported by the *Qur'an* as well as the teachings of the prophet Muhammad *SAAW*.

This is why we decided to write this series of books on frequently asked questions about raising children in North America.

It is important to note that all the questions in this series are actual questions that were asked at one time or another by workshop participants or conference and convention audience members, as well as during our live dialogues on various Websites such as *www.masnet.org* and *www.islamonline.net*.

Rather than waiting to publish a large volume covering all the questions, we decided to publish this series in small volumes to make the answers to these pressing questions immediately available to our readers.

It is also our intention, *insha'a Allah,* to continue publishing additional parts in this series, at short intervals, as we continue to receive new questions. We will try, to the extent possible, to group the questions according to the subject matter to make it easier for readers to find what they are looking for.

We would like to emphasize that our methodology in answering these questions, as has always been the case with our books, will be from an Islamic perspective drawing heavily on verses of the *Qur'an*, teachings of the prophet Muhammad *SAAW*, and events in his *Seerah*. We will also, *insha'a Allah*, draw on our wealth of practical experience, gained from countless parenting counseling sessions over the years, and our knowledge of child psychology.

This first part is divided into seven main categories covering questions related to correcting behavior, environment, Islamic identity, schooling, celebrations, sex education, and miscellaneous questions. We tried our best to respect this categorization; however, with subjects like these, there was some overlap.

We realize that this is a huge responsibility and we sincerely pray to Allah *SWT* to help us provide the right answers to these questions as well as to make this series beneficial to as many Muslim families as possible, as they seek to be the best Muslim parents for their children. We also ask Him to protect our Muslim families, our Muslim youth, our Muslim children and the entire Muslim *Ummah*.

Drs. Ekram & M. Rida Beshir

Contents

Schooling

Islamic identity

Correcting Behavior

My husband always uses the traditional methods and ways—with all their positive and negative aspects—in dealing with our children. He always says: "My opinion is right and this is the proper way to deal with the children. Our parents used to do it this way and it worked on us." I feel that this is not right. Can you please advise me what to do?

Answer   Thank you very much, Sister, for your question. To answer this, a few points must be considered. They are:

• We have to agree first that, as Muslims, our main points of reference are the Qur'an and the teachings of the prophet Muhammad *SAAW*. We should always refer any question to these original sources. No matter who used any principles before us, we have to check these principles against these main references.

• The Qur'an condemns blind imitation and suggests that believers should always find and use the proper guidelines to regulate their lives rather than follow their forefathers blindly.[1]

• Traditions are not necessarily always Islamic. Some traditions may have their origins in Islamic values while others may not, and yet others could be neutral. If the traditional methods your husband is using are based on Islamic principles, you should support him and try to use them yourself. If the traditional methods you are referring to have no basis in Islam, or go against the Islamic spirit and guidelines, it is your duty to kindly talk about this issue with your husband and remind him in a gentle manner that we should not follow these un-Islamic traditions.

---

[1] (Q43, V22-24)

• The statement that "*Our parents used to do it this way and it worked on us*" should not justify using these methods if they are not suitable for our times and environment. Ali Ibn Abi Taleb *RAA* is reported to have said: "Raise your children using ways different from the ways used with you, because they were created for times other than your times."[2] Imagine, this advice was given 14 centuries ago, when life was very slow. What about our time and age? Considering that things are changing so quickly and that the environment in North America is very different from the environment in countries where Muslims live as a majority, we need this wisdom even more, here and now.

---

[2] Imam Ali Ibn Abi Taleb enscolopedia by Muhammad Jawwad Mughneiah, Arabic, *Dar Al-Tayyar Al-Jadeed* for printing and Publications, Bayroot, Lebanon, 2004)

Can you please advise us of the most suitable way to resolve conflicts among our children? For example, my 5-year-old daughter and seven-year-old son are always fighting about who has the right to play with a certain toy. What should I do with them?

Answer Conflicts are part of life and they do happen, particularly among children (siblings), especially when they are close in age. Suitable solutions to such conflicts greatly depend on the reason for the conflict. Most of the time, in the case of young children, the conflict and fight is related to either a toy or a book that each of them want. Here are some guidelines to avoid this type of conflict:

• Set very clear rules of ownership. If the toy belongs to one child, he or she has the right to allow or not allow the other child to use it; Islam recognizes individual ownership and, at the same time, encourages sharing. Be careful, however. Do not deny anybody a right that is given to him or her by Allah SWT, even in the name of creating more sharing Muslims. This may cause sibling rivalry and resentment.

• If the toy is common, that is, it does not belong to a specific child, make sure that equal sharing is the rule. Set a specific time for each child to use the toy, for example, two to five minutes per turn, depending on the nature of the toy.

• Do not rush to solve the problem for your children. Allow them to resolve the situation themselves.

• Deal with your children equally. Do not favour one child over the other because of age, particularly if they are still young and close in age.

• Be fair in all your actions with them.

• Provide them with games and toys that can only be played by more than one person. This will teach them to cooperate and will improve their social skills by making them deal with each other.

• Tell them stories about the importance of cooperating and how important it is for siblings to bond. Make sure that the language you use is suitable for their age.

We would like to point out here that it is very important to train our children on proper Islamic conflict resolution from a young age. This will help them avoid future sibling rivalries, enmity and jealousy. At a young age, they may fight about toys and books, but if they do not learn proper conflict-resolution methodology and techniques early enough in their lives, their inability to resolve conflicts may stay with them when they grow older, and they may start fighting about more serious matters such as inheritance.

Family is the cornerstone of Muslim society. We should keep it very strong and intact by maintaining harmony among family members and by raising our children with the right Islamic guidance in every sphere of life to ensure the continuity of a strong family unit *insha' a Allah*.

 *I have two sons, six and four years old. I have noticed that my six year old is sociable and outgoing. He likes to meet new children and can make friends with them. As for my four year old, he is more withdrawn, shy, and it takes him a long time to warm up to other children and play with them. Could this be their nature, or could we have caused this to happen because of how we are treating them? Is there anything we can do to help our younger son be more sociable and get over his shyness?*

Answer   We thank the questioner for being observant and noticing these differences between her sons. This is a good quality for parents to have and it helps them recognize their children's traits early and take steps towards modifying their temperament to reach a healthy balanced point.

Every child is born with their own temperament and combination of various traits. A child could be inclined towards being sociable while his own brother could naturally be shy and withdrawn. The environment also has its own influence on a child's character. The child's temperament and surroundings mutually influence each other. A shy baby who cries and screams when someone tries to play with him would cause people around him to stay away and not play with him as much as they would with another baby who smiles at them. Another example is when a father takes his daughter to swimming classes and she fights and screams before getting into the water. That would discourage the father from taking her to such classes very often and would reinforce the withdrawn characteristic of this child.

The role of parents is to provide an environment that might help the child modify his character and be more in the middle of the road. For example, instead of following your natural instinct to avoid your shy toddler, approach him in a gentle and gradual way, or take him to play groups where he has the opportunity to play with other toddlers in the comfort of his mother's presence. Do not be discouraged by the child's crying and fussing when he is around other children. Continue to attend the play groups in order to expose him to more children. Eventually, with your assurance, he will feel more comfortable and be able to play and share in activities with other children.

Taking a toddler or preschool-aged child to the park would give him a good opportunity to get over his shyness. While he is using the play structure and being around other children, he will develop a level of comfort and confidence in his ability to deal with other children.

Parents may also enroll their children in various classes that teach them skills such as swimming, self defense, and other sports While the child's focus will be on learning these skills, he will also acquire the social skills necessary to deal with people, cultivate (reinforce) his self-confidence, and he will get over his shyness.

My son is three years old. He is generally shy. Frequently, when we go to visit other families, he becomes stubborn and stands outside refusing to enter the house. I keep telling him to go inside, but to no avail. Finally, I literally have to drag him inside the house while he is screaming. That makes me very embarrassed. Can you please advise me what to do in this case?

Answer   Your son might be naturally shy and may need time to change places and be around new people. It is good that you are taking him to visit new people and places. This will help him get over his shyness *insha'a Allah*. Here are a few suggestions to improve the situation:

• Prepare him before the visit by talking with him about the people he is going to meet and the children that he will play with. You could do this as early as one day before the visit.

• While you are driving to your friends' house, talk to him again in detail to refresh his mind about where you are going and what you are going to do once you get out of the car. For example, you could say: "When we arrive and get of the car, you might like to be the one who knocks on the door or rings the bell. When they open, we will all say *Assalamu Alaykum warahmatu Allah wabarakatuhu* and shake hands with our hosts. We will then go inside the house and sit where the host tells us. We will chat a little bit with them. After that, whenever you feel like it, you can go and play with the children in the house."

• Whenever a situation arises where he refuses to enter the host's house, stay calm. Talk to the hosts and ask their permission to stay outside for a few moments. Talk with your son calmly, assuring him that things will be all right, that you will go inside and that he can stay by your side until he feels like playing with the other children. Do not get upset with him for not wanting to go inside. If it takes too long you can tell him calmly, "I'm going inside now, and you can come in when you are ready." Enter the house, leave the door open and stay near the door where you can observe him for safety.

• Please also read the answer to the previous question for a long-term plan that you can use to help your son get over his shyness and improve his social skills.

My daughter is five years old. Every time we visit a new family that she did not know before, she insists on staying by my side during the entire visit. Even if the family has children her age, she does not play with them. Also, when I take her to the park to play, she only plays very close to me and does not use any play structure at the same time that other children are using it. She tries to stay away from any area that has other children. How can I help her get over her shyness?

Answer   Your daughter could be naturally shy. Firstly, preparing the child is a key factor in helping her warm up to new surroundings and new people. Please see the answer to the previous question for further details. Secondly, working with the child on a long-term plan to help her get over her shyness and improve her social skills is also important. Please see the answers to the previous two questions for details on this aspect. Finally, here are some additional suggestions for your specific case:

• While visiting other families, you may ask the host's permission to go with your daughter to the area where the children are playing. Stay there with her for a while, encouraging her to be part of what they are doing. If you feel that you need to be participating yourself to help your daughter be involved, you can do that, too.

• Praise your daughter for her participation, no matter how little it may be, and show your interest in the games she was playing with the children. It does not help to tell the child repeatedly to "go and play with the kids" or to say: "why aren't you playing with them?"

• Invite children to your home to play with your daughter. It is always better in the beginning to invite only one child at a time in order to prevent the visiting children from leaving your daughter out by playing only with each other. Later, when she has developed a greater ability to make friends, you can invite more children at the same time.

Use these same techniques when you take your daughter to the park. Also try to bring one of her friends with you when you go to the park.

I read in one of your books that each child tends to pick up a personality in accordance with her birth number. My question is, how would you change the personality of the "trouble making" child? Or how would you change any other personality that is not proper or desired?

Answer   First, let us clarify the issue of picking up a personality based on the child's birth number. Position within the family is not the only factor that affects a child's personality. It is only one of the factors that can affect a child's personality. Other very important factors that may have an even greater impact include family atmosphere and methods of training. Position within the family is only significant for two reasons. First, no two children will have the same position unless they are twins. Second, children do not usually want to compete for the same personality. As for the other factors, parents can make sure that the family atmosphere is the same for every child and use the same methods of training that produce positive results.

Will one of the children inevitably take on the trouble making personality because of her birth number? Of course not. But there is a possibility that one of them will do so while in the process of finding her position within the family dynamics. That is why parents must be alert and observant, and monitor the behavior of their children to detect any tendency toward bad or negative behavior. As soon as parents detect any negative behavior, they should correct it in the proper manner. We recommend using the Indicate, Educate and Train technique. This is a recommended Islamic method of correcting and changing a child's negative behavior. It consists of three steps:

1. **Indicate** clearly to the child her mistake or unacceptable behavior in a very calm but firm manner. For example, if the child was disrespectful by speaking to an older person in a rude tone of voice or by making faces at the person she was talking to, the parent who is dealing with the situation should assume that the child did not know better, and then indicate to her that this behavior is not acceptable. Do this by using an appropriate comment that suits the child's age and a firm tone of voice that is calm and not angry. It is important to emphasize here that this should be done in a very respectful way, to set an example and to show the child how you want her to behave.

2. **Educate** the child about the issue at hand using verses from the *Qur'an* and teachings of the prophet Muhammad *SAAW*. For example, when responding to disrespect, the parent could mention the following saying of the prophet Muhammad *SAAW*:

> "The one who does not have mercy on our young ones and does
> not show respect to our elders is not one of us."[3]

Referring to verses from the Qur'an and the teachings of the Prophet *SAAW* helps the child understand that our ultimate reference is to the orders of Allah *SWT*, and that even parents are expected to obey these orders. This will also help parents avoid confrontations with their children. It removes the factors that cause power struggles, since the parents are not making up the rules and imposing them on the children, but actually, both the parents and the children are following Allah's rules.

3. **Train** the child to frequently practice the correct behavior in the proper way, with your guidance. Do not expect that, by following these steps once, the child will behave appropriately all the time and not repeat the mistake. You need to repeat the process each time the child repeats the mistake or behaves in an unacceptable manner. You may have to do it more than once until it becomes a habit for the child. Training and practice makes perfect.

---

[3] Thirmidhi

For more examples and a detailed explanation of this technique, please refer to our book entitled *Parenting Skills based on the Qur'an and Sunnah.*[4]

We can also recommend that you try to identify one or more good qualities that this child has. Then make her feel good about having such qualities by encouraging her to use them. For example, if you notice that she is good at dealing with younger children, enhance this quality in her by providing her with the opportunity to interact with and supervise young children during activities at your local Islamic centre. This way, rather than resorting to mischief, she will feel valued and gain a sense of self-worth by contributing to a worthwhile cause. If you notice that the child is good at artistic expression, let her gain her sense of self-worth by contributing in this area. For example, give her the responsibility of making the posters for your next event at the mosque. This will divert her attention away from negative, trouble-making behavior. Feeling rewarded for her contribution will also help her avoid negative behaviors associated with being a troublemaker.

---

[4] Beshir, Dr. Ekram and Dr. Mohamed Rida. *Parenting Skills based on the Qur'an and Sunnah*. First edition. Beltsville, Maryland: Amana Publications, 2004.

In one of your workshops you explained the "Indicate, Educate, Follow Up" technique to correct and modify children's behavior. You pointed out, in the Educate part, that parents have to use either a verse from Qur'an or a saying of the Prophet SAAW to support their argument. However, I find it difficult to identify the relevant verses or hadeeths to use. As a matter of fact, I believe that many parents are in the same situation. Would it be enough to say to my child that this is Islamically wrong, or Muslims are not supposed to do this?

Answer   We appreciate this parent's concern and understand that it is not easy to memorize all Qur'anic verses and hadeeths related to the various virtues that we want to help our children acquire. We are not asking parents to be scholars of Islam and know every verse of the Qur'an and every hadeeth the Prophet (SAAW) ever said. Yet there is a basic minimum level of knowledge that every parent should have. In addition to the knowledge that parents need to properly practice their deen, they must also acquire the knowledge to correctly do the most important job in life—parent their children. Included in this knowledge are various issues related to the problems facing children and teenagers in this society. It is of absolute importance to instill certain Islamic concepts in your teens and develop certain characteristics in their personality to ensure that they grow up to be confident and strong Muslims. Among these concepts are: Allah SWT loves you; life is a test; our real home is in the Hereafter; Allah SWT is with you at all times; patience is a great virtue; Islam is a complete way of life; we will all meet Allah as individuals on the Day of Judgment; we are accountable for whatever we hear, see, or think about; choose your friends carefully; and so on. We refer the reader to chapter six of our book entitled *Muslim Teens*[5] for all the verses and *ahadeeth* related to these concepts. As for the Qur'anic verses related to various virtues and positive characteristics, the Islamic literature that is available on this subject is indeed plentiful. A book by the late Sheikh Muhammad Al-Ghazali entitled *The Muslim Character*, and a book by the late Sheikh Abdel-Fatah Abu Ghodah entitled *Islamic Manners* are two very good sources on this subject. Complete information about these books is listed in the reference section at the back of this book.

We do feel that it is not enough to say to our children: "This is incorrect Islamically" or "Muslims should not do this." Your children are growing up in a different environment and they need to understand the logic behind orders to be able to stand tall and strong with their differences and resist the temptation to follow the crowd. They also need to acquire this knowledge so they can answer questions directed to them by their peers in an intelligent way that does not have a negative impact on their confidence, self-esteem and personality. This, in turn, will help them feel proud to be Muslims and prevent them from compromising their *deen*.

---

[5] Beshir, Dr. Ekram and Dr. Mohamed Rida. *Muslim Teens, Today's Worry, Tomorrow's Hope, A practical Islamic Guide*. Second edition. Beltsville, Maryland: Amana Publications, 2003.

When do you ignore a child's negative behavior and when do you train him with the correct behavior?

Answer   In our view, the word ignore is not the right word to use in this situation. A better way to put it, which the reader may have meant, is to not give attention to the child's negative behavior. If the behavior is related to trivial matters—such as a young child (two to three years old) opening the refrigerator door or making a certain annoying noise just to get his parents' attention, do not give such behavior any attention. Indeed, you should ignore it. However, you have to try to find out why the child is doing this so often. Most likely, he is doing it because he is bored; he does not have anything else interesting to do. Parents should try to rectify the problem of boredom, and, *insha'a Allah*, the child's trivial negative behavior will automatically be taken care of.

If the child's behavior is hurting somebody else, you should never ignore it. You should work on correcting the behavior rather than just shout at your child and condemn his actions. The **"Indicate, Educate, and Train"** technique—as described in detail in the answer to previous questions in this book—could be effectively used to train the child to have the right behavior.

I read in one of your books about the technique of "Indicate, Educate, Follow Up and Train" to help our children improve their behavior and eliminate their shortcomings. I found it very interesting and I am trying to use it with my children. However, how can I measure the success of my attempts and how long should the training continue?

Answer   We are glad that you find this technique useful and are using it with your children. There is no single answer to this question. The training period could be as short as a few days for minor behavioural problems, and as long as three years for more important matters such as training the child to observe and establish prayer regularly. We can see this in the following statement of the Prophet *SAAW*: "Train your children to perform prayers at the age of seven and punish them for neglecting it at the age of ten."[6] The training period depends on a few factors, such as the behavior you want to change, how consistent you are in applying the technique, and the presence of other supporting factors. For example, if the behaviour you want to change is fighting with other siblings, the presence of the following factors would help in training the child to change her behavior:

• Parents must deal with all family members fairly and not favour one child over another.

• Parents must make sure that other siblings are not teasing the child in question and triggering her to start such fights.

---

[6] Sunnan Abu Dawud, and Tirmidhi

• A visual follow-up system to monitor the child's progress can be very helpful. If the child is young (around four to eight years old), a chart on the refrigerator door with check marks or stickers to be granted every time she behaves according to the required standard, or avoids doing the negative behaviour, would be very helpful. If the child is older (a pre-teen or teenager), a written contract between the child and the parent to deal with the behaviour in question works well for monitoring progress.[7]

---

[7] Refer to chapter nine of our book *Muslim Teens* for details on how to write the contract properly.

In your opinion, what is the best way to raise our children in the West?

Answer To start with, the road to successfully raising our children in the West is a rough one. It requires parents to check their concepts and distinguish between what is Islamic and what is cultural. Parents must understand that children like to imitate and fit in with whoever surrounds them. They need to build a good relationship with their children in order for the children to be willing to cooperate with and listen to them. In this sense, parents must spend time sharing activities with their children. They must also be role models in terms of their behaviour. Hence, the traditional method of telling children what to do without modeling that behavior does not work. In other words, you must practice what you preach.

Moreover, parents need to provide alternatives to the activities practiced by the mainstream culture that are not fit for their children. Take the example of a Halloween party. If parents do not want their child to go to a Halloween party, they should arrange for an alternative activity, such as visiting another family with whom your children enjoy spending time with. In this way, they will not feel that they are missing out on any fun when non-Muslim children are enjoying their holidays.[8]

---

[8] See a detailed answer on participating in Western celebrations later in this book.

Parents require three things to raise children properly in the West. Firstly, they must know the Islamic principles of raising children[9] and be familiar with the environment the children are living in. Secondly, they need wisdom in dealing with matters concerning children because different children require different approaches. Wisdom is also needed to discern how much the children are exposed to the mainstream culture and how much information they are taking from it. Thirdly, parents must put forth the effort to apply all of these principles. This can only succeed if parents consider their children among the top priorities in their lives.

The willingness of parents to change their parenting style is another very important factor that contributes to their success in raising children in the West. They must be willing to go through a self-search process to identify any negative parental behaviours they may have and make a commitment to change them into positive parental behaviours.

---

[9] For details on principles of Islamic methods of raising children see chapter two of our book entitled Parenting in the West as well as our book entitled *Parenting Skills Based on the Qur'an and Sunnah*. Both books are published by Amana Publications.

I have a difficult seven-year-old boy. He is not listening to me and my wife. He only wants to play and does not want to do his homework. What is your advice?

Answer   It is very natural for a seven-year-old child to want to play all the time. Of course, as parents, we do not want them to do this. How you give directions to your son will make a lot of difference in how he responds to you. Start the day with him on good terms by, for example, greeting him in the morning, giving him a hug and displaying lots of affection towards him.

Once these preliminary steps are taken, which strengthen the bond between parent and child, you can make an agreement with your child about one or two objectives that he must achieve that day. Let him know that once he reaches his goals, you will go with him to the park or do something else that he likes. In this way the boy will see the connection between finishing his tasks and using the rest of the time to enjoy playful activities that he likes to engage in.

Parents should not reprimand the child over and over again for not doing his work. Instead, they should follow up on his work with a chart on which he is given a star or sticker for finishing his work. Homework tasks should be done in 15- to 20-minute time slots. Then the child should be allowed ten minutes to play, rest or engage in a different activity. Lots of encouragement should be given for even the slightest improvement.

In other words, the emphasis should be on what the child can do rather than on what he cannot do.

Parents should try to answer their child's questions with a yes rather than a no. For example, if he asks: "Can I go to the park, Dad?", rather then saying: "No. You didn't finish your homework," say "Yes, we can go after you finish your homework *insha' a Allah*." This approach makes a big difference to the children.

It is important not to think of your child as a difficult child; instead, you should understand that each child needs to be dealt with in a manner that suits his personality. Maybe your son needs a lot of attention and love, and when he does not receive it, he resorts to mischievous behavior in order to get your attention.

Can you give some good reference materials on raising children in Islam? Are Dr. Seuss books acceptable from an Islamic point of view?

Answer   There is a wealth of literature in English on raising children, the first of which is the Website called Islam On-line, www.islamonline.net. We also recommend our three books: Meeting the Challenges of Parenting in the West: an Islamic Perspective; *Muslim Teens: Today's Worry and Tomorrows Hope; and Parenting Skills Based on the Qur'an and Sunnah.* All of these books are published by Amana Publications. There are other books by Muslim writers available. If you go to the Website of the Islamic Society of North America, www.isna.net, under the media mall's family section, you will find many books about parenting. Other good books that deal with parenting in North America are found on the SoundVision Website, *www.soundvision.com*, which has a family section that includes a lot of good material.

We can also recommend good books written by non-Muslims. The following are especially relevant: Teaching Your Children Values, *Teaching Your Children Responsibility,* and *How to talk so kids will listen and listen so kids can talk.* The first two books are written by Linda and Richard Eyre and the third book is by Adle Faber. One note of caution about child-rearing books written by non-Muslims is that you should make sure that the message of the book does not contradict Islamic values.

There are many children's books available in public libraries and used by teachers and parents as teaching tools, such as those written by Dr. Seuss. However, parents have a duty to screen all books before allowing their children to read them, again, to make sure that their message does not contradict any Islamic values.

In your opinion, what is the most effective punishment for a misbehaving toddler?

Answer   Dealing with toddlers is a sensitive situation. Punishment should not be used to make a toddler cooperate. Depending on the situation, parents must choose different methods. In some situations, ignoring the toddler completely is the best method. In other situations, you may have to use a time out. Physical punishment should not be used at all with toddlers. Parents should learn the Islamic principles of raising children rather than immediately resorting to punishment. Please see chapters two and four of our book entitled *Parenting in the West* as well as our book entitled *Parenting Skills Based on the Qur'an and Sunnah* (both are published by Amana Publications) for a synopsis of Islamic parenting principles and their practical applications.

From an Islamic and psychological perspective, is giving children too much attention and care when they are young good or bad for them? Also, should children be taught to be independent when they are toddlers, for example, not allowed to sleep with their parents, and so on? Some doctors recommend attachment parenting, where children are frequently cuddled, allowed to sleep with their parents, and continually given affection. Is that good or bad?

Answer   It is very important for the mental and emotional development of growing children that they receive plenty of attention from their parents, while also being taught responsibility and manners. When a parent—either the mother or the father—spends time playing with the child, for example, taking her to the park or teaching her how to ride a bicycle, all of this kind of attention will help the child gain self–confidence, acquire skills and feel loved by her parents. Meanwhile, teaching the child to be respectful of her parents, share with other friends, learn how to dress herself, and help with carrying her own toys when going to the park will make it a learning experience. It is natural for children to always seek attention; however, parents should reward the positive behavior of the child with attention and ignore the negative trivial behavior.

As for your second question, toddlers need to learn to sleep in their own beds, maybe in a separate room. The important thing here is to spend enough time with the child when she is awake. Give the child a special time slot where she receives a lot of attention before going to bed. The following are examples of activities parents can do with their children during this time slot:

• Sit with the child(ren) to eat a snack together.

• Tell a bedtime story in a playful way.

• Give them a bath, allow them to use the washroom and have a sip of water.

• Read the Qur'an to them and put your hand on each of the children's forehead while reading the Qur'an to them.

• If they are old enough, the children should be made to repeat the bedtime du'a with their parents. If the children are not old enough to repeat it, the parents should recite it aloud to them.

• Explain the meaning of the bedtime du'a as a tool to make them sleep safely and wake up comfortably.

• Play an audio tape of the Qur'an in the room, kiss them goodnight and leave the room.

With very young children, make sure that they are clean and fed before you put them to bed. This prevents them from calling you for these things once they are in bed. You can leave a toy or book that they like in bed, for them to look at until they fall asleep. You may leave on a dim light in the room so they do not feel they have to fall asleep immediately. Try to maintain a consistent bedtime, give or take an hour.

How can I deal with a jealous child who likes to have everything for himself?

Answer Treating all children with fairness and having clear, general rules for the family and children will cut down on a lot of problems related to jealousy. Providing a warm and positive family atmosphere where parents get along with each other in an honorable, kind and dignified way helps tremendously in reducing the amount of jealousy among siblings. Research indicates that when all children are satisfied with the warm affection they receive from their parents, they have less reason to begrudge the attention their parents give to their brothers and sisters.[10]

Also, a child who seems jealous sometimes needs reassurance that his parents love him. The parents will tell the child that they love him, but they have the duty of raising him to be a good person; therefore, they must still reinforce the clear rules of the house.

These are some general guidelines for reducing jealousy and sibling rivalry. If you would like a more specific answer tailored to your own case, please be more specific in your question. We will need more information about the following:

• The child's age and gender
• The number of children in the family
• The position of this child within the family (i.e., oldest, youngest, or middle)

Examples of the child's behavior, which make you identify him as a jealous child.

---

[10] *Dr. Spock's Baby and Child Care*

What is your view on physical punishment (hitting or spanking) as a way of correcting children's behavior? Is it okay to spank or hit a child when he makes a mistake? I am confused. Sometimes we get the answer that it is okay and other times that it is not okay. If it is not okay, how do you explain the hadeeth my husband refers to in which the Prophet SAAW says to teach your children to perform salah when they are seven years old and to hit them if they do not perform it when they are ten years old?

Answer   This is a very important question, particularly in the context of North America. To answer this question we have to talk about several points:

• The proper understanding of the *hadeeth* of the Prophet *SAAW*

• Other sayings of the Prophet *SAAW* related to this matter

• Whether or not the Prophet *SAAW* ever used hitting or physical punishment as a way of correcting children's behavior

• The North American environment

Let us discuss these points in detail *insha' a Allah.*

First, the proper understanding of the *hadeeth* that your husband referred to.

This *hadeeth* appears in *Sunnan* Abu Dawud as well as in the Tirmidhi collection of *hadeeth*, with minor variations. The lessons derived from this *hadeeth* are as follows:

• *Salat* is a very important ritual of purification in Islam. As a matter of fact, it is the most important pillar, after the shahada, because it links the weak creatures (humans) with their Creator, the Almighty.

• Training our children for *salat* should be taken very seriously. It may take up to **three years** to train them to observe *salat* regularly and to try their best to perfect its performance. Before parents even consider using physical punishment, they must ask themselves whether they have first spent sufficient time and energy using other, more effective training and *tarbiyah* methods—such as modeling the behavior they want to see in their child or gently advising the child—or whether they are using physical punishment on the spur of the moment to take their anger out on the child.

• In extreme cases, after parents spend up to three years properly training the child, and the child is still regularly missing *salat* or not performing it properly, parents may punish the child physically by hitting him lightly so he can understand the weight of his mistake.

• According to Islam, the responsibility of administering physical punishment must come *only after* intense and proper training have failed and *after* other methods of correcting behavior have failed. Even then, certain conditions must be fulfilled when the physical punishment is administered. The following are some of these conditions:
  – Never hit the face.
  – Avoid using your own hand; use a very light object such as a natural toothbrush (*miswak*).
  – Hitting should be very light and must never leave any mark on the child's body.

All of these conditions indicate that the hitting is very symbolic; it is meant to show that you are disappointed in the child. Again, when parents resort to this technique, they must ask themselves whether they observed all of the above conditions or simply acted out in a fit of rage.

Second, let us look at other sayings of the Prophet *SAAW* related to this matter.

"It was reported on the authority of Abu Hurairah *RAA* that the Messenger of Allah *SAAW* said: 'The strong person is not the one who wrestles but is the one who controls himself in a fit of rage.'"[11]

"Abu Mas'ud Al-Badry *RAA* reported: 'I was beating my slave with a whip when I heard a voice behind me saying: 'Abu Mas'ud, be mindful.' I did not recognize the voice due to my anger. As it approached me, I found that it was coming from the Messenger of Allah *SAAW* who was saying: 'Abu Mas'ud, be mindful. Abu Mas'ud, be mindful.' I threw the whip from my hand. The Prophet *SAAW* said: 'Be mindful Abu Mas'ud. Verily Allah has more dominance over you than you have over your slave.' Then Abu Mas'ud said: 'I would never beat my servant in the future.'"[12]

The above *ahadeeth* indicate that the prophet Muhammad *SAAW* clearly instructed his companions not to use force against anyone, especially children and women. Parents should always find other disciplinary measures and never resort to hitting or using force with their children.[13]

Third, let us examine whether the Prophet *SAAW* ever used hitting or physical punishment as a way of correcting children's behavior.

---

[11] Agreed upon
[12] Muslim
[13] Consult our books entitled *Parenting in the West, Muslim Teens* and *Parenting Skills Based on the Qur'an and Sunnah.*

"It was also reported by 'Aisha *RAA* that: 'the Messenger of Allah *SAAW* never hit with his hand either a servant or a woman, but of course he fought in the cause of Allah. He never took revenge on anyone for the torture inflicted upon him, but of course, he exacted retribution for the sake of Allah when the injunctions of Allah were violated.'" [14]

It is very clear from the above hadeeth that the Prophet of Allah *SAAW* never used force against children or women. As Muslims, we should do our best to take him as our ultimate role model; "Indeed in the Messenger of Allah you have the best example to follow for he who hopes in (the meeting with) Allah *SWT* and the Last Day and who remembers Allah *SWT* much." [15]

Finally, let us discuss the situation in North America.

In some provinces in Canada as well as some states in the United States of America, punishing children physically is against the law. It is considered child abuse. The authorities could penalize parents who use such methods by taking their children away from them and placing the children either with the Children's Aid Society or in a foster home. I do not think that any wise Muslim parent is willing to take the risk of having his child raised by a non-Muslim institution. The harm and consequences of such an act are unimaginable and should not be entertained in any way, shape or form just because the parent cannot control his or her anger.

In addition to the above arguments against using hitting or spanking to correct a child's behavior, it is clear that parents who do this are setting a bad example for their children. They are sending the message that *yes, you can settle conflicts and differences by force*. The children may use force against their own younger siblings since their parents feel it is an acceptable method.

---

[14] Muslim
[15] (Q33, V21)

There is another very important point we would like to add here. It is related to the low self-esteem of children who are insulted at home and hit or beaten by their parents. As Muslims, our goal is to raise a confident Muslim generation that can stand tall against the monumental challenges that will face it in North American society. We want a generation of proud, strong, confident Muslims. Using force as a means of *tarbiyah* will never produce such a generation.

We would also like to remind parents that using force against your children simply to vent your anger is a very serious mistake. Parents should never use force as revenge against children. After all, one of the names of the Last Day is the Day of *Qesas* (retribution or paybacks). On that day, everyone will have to pay back any rights they may have unjustly taken from somebody else. Even a horned sheep that attacked a sheep without horns during this life will be avenged by the one who was attacked. Thus, if parents hit or beat their children unjustly, they will be held accountable and may have to pay back such deeds to their children on the Day of Judgment.

Parents who think that beating their children is their birthright are seriously mistaken and are definitely committing a serious sin. Hitting children to correct their behavior is a responsibility to be exercised only in extreme cases and only as a last resort, after all other methods and techniques have failed. In addition, when a person severely misuses responsibilities such as this one, the responsibilities should be completely taken away from and not used by that person.

Environment

Our brother is married to a non-Muslim woman. He is not paying much attention to Islam or an Islamic education for his children. We are concerned about their future in North America if they do not receive clear guidance from their father regarding Islamic faith and manners. What should we do for our nephews and nieces?

Answer It is encouraging to receive such a question, indicating the concern of those sisters for their nieces and nephews. May Allah *SWT* reward them for their wonderful spirit of trying to save these Muslim children and making sure they grow up to be strong confident Muslims who observe and practice their *deen*.

There is no doubt that the role of parents is very crucial in their children's lives. Parents represent the first circle that children will encounter in their environment, and children's personalities are formed according to how their parents deal with them. The Prophet *SAAW* clearly indicated this to us in his saying:

> "All babies are born with a pure nature, and it is their parents who can change that nature and make them Jews, Christians or fire worshippers."[16]

Because of this great influence that parents have on their children, some scholars made marriage to women from the People of the Book

---

[16] Al Bukhary, Musllim, and Others

conditional upon the family's living in a Muslim-majority society [17] to ensure that the children grow up as Muslims. Our situation in North America, where Muslims live as a minority, is different. Thus, when a Muslim   man chooses to marry from among the People of the Book, he should take all precautions to ensure that his children from this marriage will be raised as Muslims. In addition to including this as part of the marriage contract with his non-Muslim wife, he must make sure that he will provide his children with all the guidance and proper support mechanisms necessary for the children's Islamic development. Parenting in North America is a huge challenge even when both parents are Muslim. It is an even greater challenge when one of them is not.

The following are some suggestions for those sisters:

• Remember that you have no control over your brother or his family. However, you may gently advise and offer subtle suggestions without being too direct or at all harsh. Do not let your genuine concern about the future of your nephews and nieces lead you to any foolish or unacceptable behavior with your sister-in-law.

• Be very kind and maintain very good relations with your brother's family. Treat your sister-in-law in the best possible way and let her see the beauty of Islam through your behavior and conduct. Remember the Qur'anic advice: "Repel (an evil) with what is best, then verily, he between whom and you there was enmity, will become as though he were a close friend,"[18] and "Allah does not forbid you to deal justly and kindly with those who do not fight against you on account of religion and who do not drive you out of your homes. Verily Allah loves those who deal with equity."[19]

---

[17] See chapter three of *Blissful Marriage, A Practical Islamic Guide* by Drs. Ekram & M. Rida Beshir. Amana publications, 2003.
[18] (Q41, V34)
[19] (Q60, V8)

• Visit your brother's family regularly and exchange gifts with them.

• Talk to your brother in a very soft, gentle and kind way to explain to him the serious consequences for him and his children if he does not provide them with the proper guidance. Mention that you are available if he needs any help or support in this matter.

• If there is a member of the community who is well respected by your brother, you could approach that community member and explain your concerns to him. Ask him to discuss the matter with your brother. He may have more influence on your brother and be able to convince him to do the right thing regarding his children's upbringing.

• Make a lot of *du'a* to Allah *SWT*, asking Him to protect your brother's children and to open your brother's heart so that he might see the seriousness of his actions and provide his children with the Islamic teachings necessary for them to grow up with strong and confident Muslim personalities.

I have two boys (ages four and two). I plan to continue my studies in Canada and I am worried that the environment there will affect my children. My older child will be in school in Canada. Canadian schools do not teach religion to students. My question has two parts. How much can the children be affected by:

>   1. The non-Muslim teachers at school? and
>   2. The environment in general?

For the most part, my wife will be staying at home looking after the children. However, I am still worried about their religion and their behavior. Do you have any advice to deal with this situation?

Answer   It is quite refreshing to see that Muslims are concerned about the affairs of their children, especially when they move to a different environment.

The importance of a proper environment for raising children cannot be overemphasized. The Prophet *SAAW* indicated in one *hadith* that human beings are born in a pure state, and it is their parents who make them Jewish, Christian or Magian (fire worshippers).[20] From among the lessons derived from this hadith, scholars have pointed out the following two:

---

[20] See the exact *hadith* reference in the previous question..

1. The environment has a great impact on a child's upbringing.

2. Parents represent the first circle of environments that a child will encounter. The influence of this circle is so significant that it can change a child's pure nature.

Other environmental circles that children face are school, neighbours, and friends (the local community). Mainstream society is, in general, represented in all the events surrounding children's lives as well as in the array of ideas and information that children are bombarded with via the media, particularly television.

Young children are very influenced by their teachers. They also like to imitate other children from school. If the teacher is promoting good values, this will not be a problem for your child. In the public school system in Canada, teachers generally treat children fairly, try to take care of the needs of each individual child, and help them learn. However, the teachers' own personal conduct may not agree with our Islamic value system, for example, their manner of dress.

The school environment also introduces children to many un-Islamic ideas, such as:

• Various celebrations (Thanksgiving, Halloween, Christmas, Valentine's Day, Easter, and so on), which seem to occur throughout the entire school year, and the whole educational program is centred on the theme of the festivity at the time.

• Classmates' behaviour (how they dress, the occasional inappropriate language they use, their general attitude, and so on).

Being aware of these dangers is a good parenting approach. It is the parents' responsibility to filter out the negative effects of this environment as part of the process of shaping the child's personality during those very important years.

Our advice is:

1. Enroll the child in a private Islamic school. Make sure you do your homework and thoroughly research the quality of education and standards of moral behavior in the school.

2. If, for any reason, an Islamic school is not the answer for you, place the child in the public school system and try to filter out the negative effects of such an environment to prevent them from reaching the child. Here are some essential techniques to apply:

a. Provide a good, warm, and cozy family environment in which everyone cares about each other. This means basing the family environment on truly Islamic values that actually represent Islam, rather than a foundation of only cultural or ethnic norms.

b. Use the true, proper Islamic methods of training for raising children[21].

c. Communicate with the children at a level they can understand and that is suitable for their age group.

d. Become actively involved at the child's school by volunteering your time as a teacher's helper during field trips and other activities.

e. Help your child participate in *show* and *tell* at their school to introduce Islamic occasions to their classmates.

---

[21] Islamic libraries are full of material on proper parenting techniques. Our books on parenting, such as *Parenting in the West, Muslim Teens*, and *Parenting skills based on the Qur'an and Sunnah* are suited more for the North American environment. See the complete reference of these books in previous sections and on the reference page.

f. Become actively involved in the Muslim community, where your children will have an opportunity to meet other Muslim children of their age and feel as though they are part of a larger community.

g. Enroll your child in a part-time Islamic school that teaches Arabic and Islamic studies; for example, an after-school program or a weekend school.

h. Work with your child on learning Arabic, Qur'an and Islamic studies at a level that you are able to teach.

The above techniques should be used by parents living in countries where Muslims are a minority, regardless of whether the child is in an Islamic or a public school. An Islamic school may make your job easier because it will push your children in the same direction that you are pushing them. If the child is not in an Islamic school, you will be pushing against the mainstream. Nevertheless, children can be, and have been, successfully raised in both situations.

I am a mother of two children who are seven and twelve years old. We live in an area where there are not many Muslim families nearby. My children want to visit their non-Muslim friends in their homes. Do you think it is a good idea for me to let them do this? Please advise me what to do.

Answer The need for friends and acquaintances is natural for children. Parents should acknowledge this need and try to satisfy it to the best of their ability. They should also teach their children the proper criteria for selecting friends. It was reported by Abu Hurairah *RAA* that the Prophet Muhammad *SAAW* said: "A man follows the religion of his closest friend, so each one should consider whom he makes his friend."[22] In another narration, Abu Musa al-Ash'ari *RAA* heard the Messenger of Allah *SAAW* saying: "Good company and bad company are like the owner of musk and the iron smith. The owner of the musk will either offer you some musk free of charge, or you will buy it from him or smell its pleasant odour. As for the iron smith, either he will burn your clothes, or you will have to smell the repugnant smell of the iron."[23]

It is recommended that parents satisfy their children's need for friends by making them befriend other Muslim children of the same age, even if this means enduring some inconveniences, such as driving to the other side of the city. If this is absolutely unattainable, there are a few important points you must take into consideration before allowing them to visit non-Muslim friends in their homes. These are:

---

[22] Muslim
[23] Agreed upon

* Make sure that the effect of those friends on your children is going to be positive.

* Make sure that the environment at their home is safe; the safety of your children should never be compromised. For example, from the physical safety point of view, the kids aren't allowed to play with knives, sharp objects, or swim in a pool unsupervised. As from the moral safety point of view, the kids aren't allowed to watch T.V. unsupervised or smoke cigarettes as well as the parents are not just sitting around drinking beer. As a mother, you could visit this family, get to know them and have an idea about their home environment before allowing your child to visit their home.

* Ensure that one of the parents is going to be home during the visit. If your children are girls, make sure that the mother is home and that no boys are in the house while your girls are visiting. If your children are boys, make sure that either the father or the mother is home during the visit.

* Give your children clear instructions about what they should be careful of during the visit. Tell them that, if they ever feel uncomfortable at any time for any reason, they should call you right away to have you pick them up.

* Be on the lookout for any change in your child's behavior after such visits to make sure that the visits are not having a negative impact on your child. This will prevent you from having to work hard to reverse any negative effects.

* If you feel that any of the above criteria are not met or that the safety of your child may be compromised, it might be a better idea to host your child's friends at your house.

If the above criteria are not met, and you decide not to allow your children to visit their friends at their homes, make sure that you clearly explain to your children the reasons why you made such a decision. Safety should come at the top of your explanation list, and you should acknowledge your children's need to be with their friends.

As parents, how can we counter the hundreds of messages coming to our children from schools, the media and society concerning un-Islamic values?

Answer   The first issue is that the environment can have very detrimental effects on our efforts to raise our children. The Prophet *SAAW* stated that all babies are born with a pure nature, and it is their parents (the first circle of environments) who can change this nature and make them either Jewish, Christian, or fire worshippers. This shows how influential the environment is on our children.

Parents represent the first circle of environments that our children are subjected to. In North America, schools and society at large represent another circle affecting our children. Most of the time, the messages they receive from their peers at school and from the media are against Islamic values. Parents have a role in ensuring a proper environment and providing a support system for their children to help them counter these un-Islamic messages. Therefore, if your child is in a public school, you should always try to visit the school to inform the school administration about the needs of Muslim children: make them aware of various Islamic occasions such as *Ramadan* and *Eid*, as well as their dietary requirements. Parents can also participate with their children in classroom activities such as show and tell, which will give them an opportunity to correct some misconceptions about Islam. You could arrange information displays about Islam, in an open house format, for example. For this to be effective, parents should occasionally volunteer for school activities.

Other things you can do is to organize camps for Muslim youth where they can live Islam with other Muslim children.

Before children will be willing to listen, parents must have a very good relationship with them. Basically, it is best not to be critical. Instead, be encouraging with the children and be involved in their lives and activities, whether at home or in the community. Whenever they are getting a different message from outside, express your love to them and explain the wisdom behind your objections to that message. And be happy when they come to you with questions.

How can I find good children's magazines, books, and colouring books that have an Islamic theme?

Answer   The best way to find these is to attend some of the national conventions and go to their bazaars.

• The Islamic Society of North America (ISNA) convention takes place every year in September, on Labor Day weekend.

• The Muslim American Society (MAS) and the Islamic Circle of North America (ICNA) together hold two conventions annually, one on the Fourth of July weekend and the other during the Christmas holidays in December.

Another way is to visit the following Websites, which have good educational material for children:

> • ISNA's Media Mall: www.isna.com
> • Noor Art: www.noorart.com
> • Astrolabe: www.astrolabe.com
> • Multivisions Extra Inc.: www.multivisionsinc.com
> • SoundVision: www.soundvision.com
> • Amana Publications: www.amana-publications.com
> • Muslim American Society Council of Islamic Schools
>   (MAS CIS): www.masnet.org/school.asp
> • International Board of Educational Research and Resources
>   (IBERR) at http://www.iberr.org/

After they get married, do children have to live in their parents' home if that is what the parents wish? Can they move out but still maintain a close relationship?

Answer   Children have to provide good company to their parents, look after them, and try to make their parents pleased with them. Children are also entitled to their own lives. These two sets of rights and responsibilities must be balanced, and this can be done in different ways.

One way is for the children to live nearby but keep in touch with the parents to make sure all their needs are fulfilled. As the child in this situation, if you move out, be gentle with the move, reassure your parents that you love them, that you are going to be part of their lives, and be patient with them as they adjust to the idea.

Do you advise Muslims to enroll their children in non-Muslim activities such as soccer and baseball leagues in the city?

Answer It is very important for children to be involved in various activities and to live an active lifestyle, which may include sports or being with other children. The best solution is for parents to provide these activities for their children in an Islamic environment, particularly when the children are still vulnerable and in the early stages of development.

In cases where this is not possible, parents may research activities run by non-Muslim groups. If your research indicates that the behavior and language used by the non-Muslim children is appropriate and decent, there is no harm in allowing your children to participate in those activities. An exception would be if the activity is co-ed and the children are in their pre-teen (nine years old and up) and teenage years.

While your children are participating in these activities, you should monitor and assess any changes in their behavior. If you notice that these changes are negative, then you should try to modify this behavior through discussion and explanation. If this negative behavior persists, you should consider withdrawing the child from these activities if they are the cause of the problem.

Before each activity session with the non-Muslims, you should encourage your children to observe Islamic behavior during their interaction with non-Muslims, such as wearing proper attire, doing their prayers during breaks, and conducting themselves with appropriate Islamic manners. Remind them that Allah *SWT* will reward them for their efforts and for being good models of Islam in front of non-Muslims.

How important is it to expose toddlers to other children who are their age or older? What should parents do if they sense that their children are picking up bad habits from other children?

Answer   It is important for a toddler to be exposed to other children. This is even more important if the child is the first born or does not have siblings close to his age. When children associate and interact with children of the same age, or nearly the same age, they have the opportunity to learn important social skills. If they are not given this opportunity at an early age, they may not sufficiently develop their social skills. When children play or even fight with each other they are acquiring negotiation skills that are essential for their social well-being. If they are not exposed to challenges at an early age, they may fail to conduct themselves in a proper and socially effective manner when they eventually go to school or interact with other children later.

As for your second question, parents are responsible for ensuring the safety and well-being of their children. If they leave them with someone, they should ensure that the environment is safe. With respect to toddlers interacting with other toddlers and picking up bad habits, we see that these bad habits are usually nothing worse than hitting, using inappropriate language, or being wild and unruly. None of these habits or behaviours are serious enough in toddlers to stop parents from letting their children interact with others.

If there are other toddlers whom your child can interact with as an alternative, you should have your child play with them instead. But if there is no satisfactory alternative in terms of other toddlers or children, you should not deny your child the chance to interact with other children; it is more important for them to develop socially through interaction. If your child is picking up bad habits from other children you should tell your child firmly that such behaviours are unacceptable.

How you communicate this message is as important as the message itself. Therefore, when you tell your child to stop an unacceptable behavior, you should be completely free from doing other tasks while you communicate this message to your child. Moreover, it is important to stop the child immediately, face her and give her your full attention while communicating that message to her.

Another way to get rid of bad habits is to read through children's books that deal with moral behavior, or to make up a story that deals with that particular bad habit. When the child repeats a bad habit, it is important for the parent to remind her of the character in the story (refer to chapter four of our book entitled *Parenting in the West* for details on how to use stories to correct bad habits; and the recently published book by Hoda Beshir, *Parenting through Storytelling*). In addition, if the child engages in bad behavior, she should be made to feel the natural consequences of that behavior by being deprived of the activity she was doing or with a timeout.

These days, in which Muslims are the object of suspicion, especially here in the U.S., how can we convince our children that racism and prejudice are wrong, particularly when they hear insults and bad things about Muslims at school?

Answer   Being a Muslim means that we should act Islamically under all circumstances and be role models of goodness despite any injustices perpetrated against us. This is obvious in the case of the Prophet *SAAW* and his companions in the challenges they faced from the non-believers. One example of this conduct is when a Muslim family (Aal-Yasir) was being physically tortured. Whenever the Prophet *SAAW* passed by them, he would urge them to be patient.

When our children interact with people from Western cultures or at school, they must be encouraged to continue acting according to Islamic values and not to resort to foolish behaviour if they are unfairly provoked by others. However, we do not mean that our Muslim children should be passive, but rather that they should accept the challenge they are faced with and try to correct the problem through constructive means, such as discussion. By acting in this manner, they will incur the support of Allah *SWT* and bring about changes in the people around them, even though it may take time to see the results.

Parents should play an active role in supporting their children by talking with the school administration and presenting the Islamic stance on issues of injustice and racism through interactive sessions with the school community. Parents should explain to their children that not all Americans support this negative attitude. You can expose your children to a more positive side of American culture by having them interact with more friendly and supportive Americans and by showing them news articles, such as those found in *The Guardian* of UK and at http://www.guardian.co.uk/guardian and *The Independent* also of UK at http://news.independent.co.uk/ The articles written by Robert Fisk as well as articles in the Orlando centennial could also be of great help. The Islamic circle of North America website (ICNA) has a great collection of these articles at http://www.icna.com/

For more positive news articles please, also check www.isna.net, and www.masnet.org. You should expose your children to opinion polls indicating that a large percentage of Americans are against these types of injustice and prejudice. This way, the children will see that the situation is not as bleak as it seems.

How do we balance the need to live an Islamic lifestyle with the need to interact in Canadian society?

Answer   For parents to balance an Islamic personality with interactions in mainstream, non-Muslim, Canadian society, they must raise their children to have a strong Islamic identity and self-confidence. This way, the children will find it possible to mix with non-Muslims and excuse themselves when an un-Islamic act is taking place. For example, if a child is at recess at school and hears his friends saying swear words, he will be able to either tell them not to say those words in front of him, or he will excuse himself and leave the group temporarily. So the child will continue mixing with the non-Muslim mainstream, but whenever something un-Islamic is taking place, he will put his Islamic identity ahead of being with his friends. That takes self-confidence from the child's side and a very close relationship with his parents. A close relationship means that the parents sit with the child, listen to what went on during the day when he was out, and provide him with comfort and support.

As an alternative, parents can also provide Muslim groups where he can mix more with children of his own age who share the same Islamic values. Plenty of practical tips on how parents can make sure that their children grow up with strong Islamic confidence can be found in chapter one of the book entitled *Meeting the Challenge of Parenting in the West*, and chapter four of the book entitled *Muslim Teens*.[24]

---

[24] See details in the reference section at the end.

We are new Muslims, having converted just 3 1/2 months ago, and I am having difficulty in finding a balance to prevent our children from regretting their own choice to convert. My daughter has just entered junior high and she proudly started wearing the hijab to school even though she is only 12. She met some girls who were raised as Muslims since birth, and they do not wear the hijab. My question is, how can I encourage my daughter to wear her hijab when the girls who were raised as Muslims do not? Now she does not wear it and she wants to attend school dances with them at night. I will not permit this because I think she is too young to attend dances at night, but they only remain too young for a period of time. What should I do?

Answer   We commend this sister for making the right decision and trying to make her children adhere to Islamic values.

As for how to help your children follow Islamic rules, keep searching for families who are committed to Islam and who apply its rules, even if their children do not attend your daughter's school. You could meet such families through the mosque in your town or city, or even through Islamic conferences. If you meet families who are committed to Islam, help your children make friends with their children by staying in touch with them, either on a weekly basis if they live in the same city or on a yearly basis if you meet them through conferences. Of course, they can e-mail each other and share their experiences.

Explain to your children that not all Muslims are fully dedicated to Islam, but that you would like them to be around those who are because those are the people of Paradise *insha' a Allah*. Getting your children to participate in youth groups in your area and attend Islamic camps during summer vacation and winter break would also help tremendously.

Keep a close relationship between you and your children; listen to the reasons they give for why they want to go to the dances. Explain to them that dances are not going to help them be good people, and that Allah *SWT* has a much better reward for them in Paradise. Keep working on it and do not feel insecure if their pain does not go away quickly, as long as you are reassuring them and doing the abovementioned things.

A twelve year old is at the beginning of adolescence, and the most important thing for her is the approval of her peers. As a mother, you should do some reading to understand the changes that take place during adolescence and how to treat her Islamically. This will be of great help in dealing with the problem. Detailed information can be found in our book entitled *Muslim Teens*.

Schooling

How do you deal with dating problems in high schools? Is there any possibility of handling the problem as a mother or as a teacher? I am both.

Answer   For Muslim teens who are attending high school surrounded by fellow students who are dating and attending dances, it is very difficult to be different and not do what everyone else is doing. The Muslim youth need to be involved in other groups of people their own age who are living by the rules of the Islamic value system. They can do this by attending camps and youth groups on a regular basis and by maintaining a close relationship with an adult in their life, preferably their parents or the youth group leader. They also need to participate in activities such as hiking, nature trips, sports, and so on.

Therefore, as a teacher and mother, you can ensure that such a youth group exists in your area. Perhaps you can lead one or facilitate the formation of one.

Dialogue with your teens in a very calm and loving way about the dangerous situation that Muslims can get into because of dating. Do this in a way that touches their hearts, as the Prophet *SAAW* did with the young man who had asked him permission to fornicate. Have an open heart, listen, dialogue and suspend your judgment when you deal with this age group.

Give the teens explanations and ask them: "What is the purpose of dating during the teenage years?" The purpose of a man and a woman getting to know each other should be marriage. Since teenagers are still very young, there is really no purpose for them to start this so early. When youth start dating, many times they end up having a baby, and that baby will likely grow up without one of his or her parents. This is not fair to the baby, and no one should allow this to happen. When people are ready for marriage and can accept the responsibilities of it, such as supporting themselves financially and being able to care for their children, only then can they start pursuing marriage in the proper way.

My question is regarding school for young children. Do you think it is a good idea to put children in a preschool program starting when they are two and a half years old, or is it better for them to stay with their mother until they are a little older? What do you believe is better for their psychological and mental development? I do take my daughter to group programs in the community so she can interact with other children, but I want to know if her going to school alone in a more structured setting is a good idea?

Answer   For now, it is good to take your two-and-a-half-year-old daughter to a playgroup twice or more a week so she can interact with other children in the presence and safety of her mother.

Starting when she is three years old, taking her for half a day of school two to three times a week is also a good idea. She will learn how to interact with other children, how to manage on her own, and how to make the necessary adjustments early in her life. However, it is important to emphasize the following points:

• Two to three times a week is sufficient for children this age. Do not overdo it by sending the child every day.

• Mother has to follow up regularly and stay closely in touch with the school. Perhaps she can do this by volunteering frequently and listening attentively to the child's message about her experience at school. This will put the mother in a better position to evaluate the school environment and make sure that the school activities are meeting her child's needs. Also, by being closely in touch with the school, the mother can explain things to the child that the child might otherwise misinterpret, as well as encourage and support her daughter in areas of weakness that she might discover.

Our young daughters in middle and high school are faced with a conflict between the school culture and what we require from them to keep the character of modesty and decency and to act upon it. In the school culture, they are trained to express their point of view and be assertive. They also feel the pressure of wanting to be like everybody else in how they dress and present themselves. However, we are teaching them to practice hayaa' and dress modestly according to the Islamic dress code. None of them want to wear jilbabs or skirts while going to middle or high school. If they cannot wear tight blouses and stretch pants, they would go for very baggy pants and shirts. How can I get my daughter to dress Islamically, conduct herself modestly, and still survive the peer pressure during middle and high school?

Answer   This question addresses two main issues, namely, the issue of *hayaa'*, and the issue of peer pressure on Muslim teens in middle school and high school.

First, let us try to clarify the meaning and implications of *hayaa'*. This word encompasses modesty, decency, bashfulness and healthy shyness. We use the Arabic word *hayaa'* because no single word in the English language is equivalent to this Islamic term. *Hayaa'* is an important character in Islam, as indicated by the Prophet *SAAW*, who said: "For every deen, there is a predominant character, and the predominant character of Islam is *hayaa'*."[25] It means that people should shy away from doing anything that is indecent, and always conduct themselves in a modest manner. The highest level of *hayaa'* is *hayaa'* from Allah *SWT*, in which a person is always careful that Allah *SWT* never sees him doing something that may displease Allah *SWT*, to the extent that the person's

---

[25] Malik

tastes, likings and dislikings are defined by what pleases Allah *SWT*. This can only be achieved through striving and exerting effort to improve one's relationship with Allah *SWT*. By building such a high level of *hayaa'* from Allah *SWT* and by following the great *fiqhi* rule of *choosing the lesser of two evils*, parents can help their children and teenagers ultimately adhere to Islamic values, one of which is dressing modestly.

Choosing the lesser of two evils is a great rule in Islamic jurisprudence, deduced by scholars from the practices of the Prophet *SAAW* and from the teachings of the Qur'an. This rule should be understood properly and used and applied wisely by parents in the North American environment. We have come across many cases in which committed Muslim parents miserably failed to use this rule and ended up driving their children away from Islam. Some of those children became completely lost to mainstream North American society, while others are at an unacceptable level of Islamic commitment and practice. We have also come across parents who were wise enough to use this rule properly and, with the help of Allah *SWT*, protected their children from deviating from Islam. Most of those children are at a very good level of commitment to Islam and are very good, practicing Muslims now *alhamdulillah*. Let us illustrate what we mean by the following example, which is specifically related to the issue of clothing:

When it comes time for a young woman to wear *hijab*, some parents insist that she wear long, loose dresses (*jilbabs*) or skirts and a long *khimar* right away. While this may be closer to the full *hijab*, it is often an extreme change for the young woman to make, and she may not feel ready for it. In some cases we have seen, this has caused the young woman to completely deviate from Islam, which is clearly the greater harm. In other cases, the parents see that the daughter does not feel ready to make a complete change, and they allow her to start by wearing loose pants and loose, long-sleeved shirts with her headscarf. While this is the minimum for *hijab*, it is better that the young woman starts off gradually and make the change to looser clothing when she is ready. This way, we have avoided the greater harm of deviation by allowing the lesser harm of a temporary, lower level of *hijab*. While the young woman is in this first stage of wearing *hijab*, the parents should help her strengthen her belief so that she may eventually feel ready to move up to the next level.

Following this principle will help teens feel that Islam makes sense and does not enforce or impose things on people without preparing them to take on huge responsibilities. This will increase your teenager's commitment to Islam, from the level of knowledge to the level of complete conviction that it is the right way to follow *insha'a Allah*.

I am a teacher at an Islamic school. It happens that my son, who is in second grade, is a student in my classroom this year. I am having trouble with this situation because he often breaks the rules. I expect him to follow the class rules, and I follow up by applying the consequences on him when he breaks them. However, he continues to break the rules. What would you suggest that I do?

Answer Your son probably feels awkward about having his mother as his teacher. In the school environment, where your attention is distributed among all the children in class, your son might feel insecure and try to get your undivided attention with what seems to be misbehaviour.

We suggest that you talk to your son openly at home to assure him that your role as his mother is solid and firm. You can start a conversation by asking him: "What is it like for you at school this year? I feel awkward being your teacher. You know, sometimes, I feel like I want to hug you and kiss you right in the middle of the classroom. Then, I remember, 'Oh, no, I'm your teacher now.' I tell myself, 'I'll wait until we go home and then I'll give you a big hug.' You know, I love you so much. I know you are a good boy and you are also a good student. Come now and give me a big hug and let us prepare dinner together."

The next morning, on your way to school, talk with your son again, saying something like: "Let us have our little secret. You and I are going to remember to follow the rules at school today and we will cook dinner together again when we go home. You helped me so much yesterday. Don't tell anybody about our little secret."

Your son will always need your assurance and follow-up through the school year, because the situation is not easy on him. The two roles you are playing, mother and teacher at the same time, can be very confusing for him.

We are glad that you enforce the rules and expect your son to follow them. This is a healthy attitude, unlike that of other teachers who would favour their son in the classroom with extra attention, because they themselves are confused between their roles as mother and teacher.

What is the best way for us to follow up on our child's homework? Sometimes we are very busy and do not have any time to do this. Do you have any suggestions?

Answer   Parents can make an agreement with their child that the child can complete her homework every night and show it to her parents by a certain time in the evening, and that if she needs help, she must ask for it. This agreement will include either a follow-up chart, for younger children, or a contract between the parent and child, for older children and teenagers. Using the chart, the parent and child will decide what reward(s) the child will receive if she sticks to the agreement, or what consequences she will have or privileges she will lose if she breaks the agreement. The parents still have to follow up with the child, but this will make it easier than simply telling her to do her homework.

A follow-up chart works better for children in grades one through five, and a contract works better for children in grades six and up. A detailed sample on how to prepare a contract between you and your child can be found in chapter nine of our book entitled Muslim Teens, published by Amana Publications.

Is it safe to send our children to a public school in junior high?

Answer   We cannot say that it is safe for parents to send their children to junior high school without taking certain precautions. Parents must be very involved, and if there is an Islamic junior high in the area, it is better to send them there.

If there is no Islamic junior high school in your area, and you have to send your child to a public school, it is very important that you research the situation thoroughly. Visit the school and learn about the environment of the school as much as you can, because some schools are safer than others, depending on where you live.

After doing your research, if you decide to send your child to a public school, you need to maintain a close relationship with your child so that you remain aware of what is going on at school and can compensate for the negative aspects by instilling good Islamic values in him. You can do this by enrolling him in Islamic camps, weekend religious schools, and positive youth group activities, such as balanced study circles and sports teams in your community.

During a life dialogue on www.masnet.org, in one of your answers, you said that some schools are safer than others. When do you describe a school as "safe"?

Answer   We can easily describe a school as safe when there is no drug trafficking taking place and no violence. Also, if the school shows acceptance of cultural differences and promotes respect for everybody, then the school is safe.

However, safety alone is not reason enough for us to put our children in a public school. Parents still have a lot of work to do with their teens to ensure that they do not fully assimilate with the mainstream culture but rather intelligently integrate into it. This means that they must be strong enough to keep their Islamic identity and that they do not mind being different and distinguished from the mainstream.

Recently I followed one of your life dialogues on www.masorg.net and I felt that you do not recommend the public school system. Do you mean that schools in the West have some problems that may affect our Muslim families here?

Answer   Yes, public schools in the West have some problems, mainly related to the environment and the popular, mainstream culture of this society. This is normal for all minority groups who have a different value system.

Some of these problems can be related to celebrations such as Christmas, Halloween and Valentine's Day. Others could be regarding relations between the genders, school dances, private parties, boyfriend and girlfriend issues and clothing. In chapter three of our book *Meeting the Challenge of Parenting in the West, An Islamic Perspective,* which is dedicated to discussing how the environment affects our children, we describe these problems in detail and suggest ways to avoid the negative effects that these problems can have on our children. Additional information on the problems facing Muslim teens in the public school system can also be found in our book entitled *Muslim Teens: Today's Worry, Tomorrow's Hope.*

As a mother, I am going to be living in the U.S. for a short period of time, just one year. My daughter is at the age that she will be attending her first preschool. Would sending her to a public school have a negative effect on her identity and language acquisition?

Answer   If you are staying in the U.S. for only one year, and you, as the mother, can become involved a little bit at your daughter's school, there should be no harm to her identity or language acquisition. This is assuming that you will also address issues such as Christmas and Halloween, explain to the child that these holidays are not Islamic and that we do not celebrate them, and make Eid the real celebration.[26]

---

[26] See the section on celebrations later in this book for details on how Muslim parents can deal with various Western celebrations.

Islamic Identity

Asalamu alaykum. I am a newly practicing sister. I have a 14-month-old baby boy and would like to raise him Islamically. Can you please recommend a book or Website that covers how I should raise my child at this young age and deal with all the dilemmas that arise with a 14-month-old baby?

Also, what is your view on children watching cartoons in English, and where can I obtain Islamic cartoons?

My last question is about your thoughts on young children and computers, from an Islamic perspective. I am completing a dissertation that involves looking at software for toddlers and gender differences. For this dissertation, I will be creating software applications for children. I would like to produce a package that teaches Islam to young children. What is the Islamic view of children and computers? I have asked a lot of questions. I hope you can answer them for me.

Answer *Wa alaykum asalaam*, Sister. First, we would like to congratulate you for practicing the *deen*. We ask that Allah *SWT* give you courage and patience in doing so and that He reward you with *jannah insha'a* Allah.

Your question basically consists of three parts. Let us deal with them one at a time, *insha'a* Allah.

Your first question is related to reference materials to help you raise your 14-month-old boy according to Islamic principles of parenting. For this, we can direct you to the following:

• Books entitled *Meeting the Challenge of Parenting in the West, An Islamic Perspective* and *Parenting Skills Based on the Qur'an and Sunnah* by Drs. Ekram and Mohamed Rida Beshir, published in the U.S. by Amana publications. Although these books do not exclusively target parenting of young children, the Islamic principles and practical examples presented in the books are applicable to all ages. These books are simple, easy to read, and enhanced with many practical examples of how to apply the principles with your children. They also contain a list of good references. These books have received excellent reviews from many readers. We recommend that you check out these reviews on the www.amazon.com Website. If you are interested, you may order the books directly from the publisher, either via their Website at www.amana-publications.com or by calling (301) 595-5888.

• The *American Muslim Magazine* published by the Muslim American Society. This magazine has a wonderful family section that includes plenty of good articles on parenting according to Islam. You can access most of the issues on-line at www.masnet.org by following the *American Muslim Magazine* link.

• For answers to questions regarding this specific age group (14 months old), consult the parenting section of www.islamonline.com.

• For parenting articles in general, consult www.soundvision.com.

• Search the Internet, but be careful about the sources and screen the material you find. Try to use material written mainly by Muslim scholars.

Your second question is about our view on children watching cartoons in English, and how to obtain Islamic cartoons. Here are our views:

• Watching TV in general, and children under three years of age watching cartoons, are very sensitive and controversial issues, and neither are recommended.

• Research indicates that it is not healthy for children under three years of age to watch TV. It affects their ability to focus in later years.

• It is much better for children at this age to play with real toys than to watch images on a screen. It is also extremely important for them to spend enough time interacting with their parents.

• Non-Islamic cartoons could be watched after the age of three, provided that the parents supervise the child and make sure that the cartoon is suitable. Parents have to be very selective in what they allow their children to watch.

• Again, research indicates that a great number of non-Islamic cartoons include violence, which has very harmful effects, especially on boys, in later years of their life.

• Limited, supervised viewing is always recommended regardless of whether the cartoon is non-Islamic or Islamic.

• A variety of Islamic cartoons and children's videos are currently available through many Websites, such as:
- www.soundvision.com
- www.isna.net [Check the media mall]
- www.astrolabe.com
- www.icna.com

Most of these Websites belong to Islamic producers or organizations located mainly in North America. They may also have representatives carrying their products in Europe. One European name that comes to mind is "The Islamic Foundations of UK."

Your third question is about children using computers. Here is what we think:

• Computers and TV are merely tools. They are not prohibited in and of themselves. They can be used for either a good cause or a bad cause. How they are used is what determines whether they are prohibited or allowed. Islam provides proper guidelines that should be followed, even for permissible and allowed matters. Here are some of the key guidelines:

- The material presented (programs, in the case of TV, and software applications, in the case of computers) should be Islamically acceptable and suitable.

– Even material that is allowed should not be used excessively and should not waste the user's time or divert attention from more important matters, such as personal well-being and proper Islamic development.

• Having said this, we think that using computers by following the above guidelines is much better for children than watching TV. While using a computer application, the child must interact with it regularly for the application to work. This is stimulating and can support the child's development, unlike TV programs, which do not require the child to interact at all and therefore leave the child completely passive.

• Children can start using computers with the appropriate software programs when they are as young as two years old.

• It would be wonderful if you could produce a software package such as the one you mentioned. Islamic libraries for children are in great need of such products. This kind of package would certainly help the new Muslim generation living in the West. It would serve a very important purpose. It is a great project and we hope you can get all the help you need from all dedicated Muslims. Some of the Websites we mentioned above also produce Islamic software for children.

My friend and I had a discussion about praising children. I believe that it is healthy to frequently give positive remarks to children, while she believes that doing this spoils children and makes them arrogant and full of themselves. Can you please advise us on this matter? Jazakum Allahu Khayran.

Answer *Jazakum Allahu Khayran*, Sister, for asking this question. This discussion is very common among Muslim parents, and your question has been raised several times during our Positive Parenting Skills workshops.

Actually, both of you hold part of the truth. The full truth and the proper way of dealing with this matter are a combination. In addition to certain precautions that should be taken and observed by parents to prevent children from becoming arrogant due to continuous praise, we have some suggestions about what parents can do to properly give their children positive reinforcement.

• It is better to make positive comments on a regular basis specifically in reaction to something good that the child has done (for example, good behaviour) rather than praise the child all the time for no reason. For example, if your son is helping his sister with her homework, you can say: "*Masha'a* Allah. I like this. You are a helpful person and Allah *SWT* will reward you for your good deed, *insha'a* Allah." Or when your six-year-old daughter is dressed in new clothes you could say: "That looks nice on you." These are positive comments that make our children feel good, and it is recommended that every parent make such encouraging comments to their children. On the other hand, when parents repeatedly praise their children with comments such as: "You are so beautiful," or "You are the best child in the family," this could make the children become full of themselves and could promote arrogance in their personality.

• At the same time, parents should teach and train their children to be responsible. They should not accept misbehaviour, which should be dealt with promptly using the "Indicate, Educate and Train" techniques, which are described in detail in a previous chapter entitled "Correcting Behaviour."[27]

• Parents should remind their children that, whenever we are blessed with certain talents, we should be grateful to Allah *SWT*. This way, our good deeds will be accepted, and we will be rewarded for using our talents to perform any deed or to act in any way that is in line with Islamic values.

• Parents must also teach their children the virtues of being modest and humble. The stories of the Prophet Muhammad *SAAW* are the most beautiful tools to help our children realize the importance of these wonderful qualities.

Following the above tips could *insha'a* Allah help us make our children feel good when they are being praised for their positive actions, and simultaneously ensure that they do not become arrogant or full of themselves.

---

[27] Dr. Ekram and Dr. M Rida Beshir *Positive Parenting Skills based on the Qur'an and Sunnah*. Amana publications, 2004.

I have a three-and-a-half-year-old boy and I am starting to tell him about Allah. I tell him that we pray to thank Allah for all the good things He gives us. Two days ago, my son had a nightmare so I told him that, if we read the Qur'an together before sleeping, he will be protected from the animals that bite him in his nightmare. My husband thinks it is too early to tell him all that. I would like my husband to read something to convince him that it is not too early, as long as I am not mentioning hell or devils or anything like that. I would appreciate your help.

Answer It is never too early to teach our children about Allah because the Prophet *SAAW* asked us to start doing this from day one by giving the *adhan* (the call to prayer) in their right ear and the *iqamah* (the call to start the prayer) in their left ear as soon as they are born. The very first words they should hear are about Allah *SWT*. This should continue throughout the development of the child.

When we teach our children about Allah *SWT* as the Creator, the One who provides for us and the One who protects us, these concepts become ingrained in the children's psyche and become an integral part of their personality and belief. Therefore, we have every reason to teach our children about Allah *SWT* from a very early age. Although there is no specific *hadith* or injunction that we can think of right now in regards to teaching toddlers about evil things, we have been advised by the Prophet *SAAW* that we should do the *ruqqiyah* for everyone, including newborn babies, to protect them from evil things. Part of ruqqiyah is to read the last three surahs of the Qur'an, which include seeking refuge in Allah *SWT* from evil forces and *shaytan*.

Another piece of advice is that, whenever parents talk to their children about Allah *SWT*, they must put more emphasis on the compassionate attributes of Allah *SWT*, such as mercy, kindness, gentleness and forgiveness, particularly with very young children. This does not mean that we do not tell them about Allah's punishment for those who do evil, but we do not dwell on it when the children are very young. When this punishment is mentioned, it should be mentioned in an indirect way, by talking about someone else who has been deprived of the mercy of Allah *SWT*.

Furthermore, at bedtime we should spend some time with our children in a playful way, read them nice stories and avoid speaking about evil things. In regards to your son's nightmares, you could say: "We are going to read the Qur'an, and *insha' a* Allah you will see nice beautiful dreams" instead of talking specifically about protection from the animals that will bite him.

I read in one of your books that providing an active lifestyle is very important to our children's and teenagers' love for Islam. In our community, we do not have many activities to attract youth and teens. What should we do?

Answer Yes, providing active lifestyle for our children and youth is a very important part of their healthy and balanced development. Ensuring that activities are available is the responsibility of parents and concerned community members. There is no excuse whatsoever for not providing activities for our children and youth. Failure to do this may have a detrimental effect on their lives when they grow older. An active lifestyle should include their lives at home, their lives within the community, and their lives among mainstream society.

• At home, parents should always have a balanced schedule to allow the children to enjoy certain games and activities in addition to carrying out duties and chores. Family outings, picnics, playing on the play structure at the park, and registering for swimming classes are a small sample of the kind of activities that families can do together.

• Community and Islamic centres should, through their youth committees and departments, organize activities such as sports competitions (soccer, basketball, and so on). Organized and structured activities are of great help to teens and youth. If the community is small or unable to organize activities on its own, the following can be done:

– Individuals and families should use facilities that already exist in the community, especially when the children are young. In addition, we should not feel shy about using community facilities that are run by non-Muslims because we are also part of this society, and as tax-paying members of our communities, we should also utilize the facilities available to us.

– Muslim sisters or Muslim brothers can reserve community facilities as a group. Such groups must follow the rules and can also enjoy using such facilities without violating any Islamic principles.

– Parents can get together and start their own activities.

Sex Education

I am a father of three children, ages five, three and two. My wife and I are doing our best to raise our children in a balanced Islamic way. Could you tell us what is the appropriate age at which parents should start talking to and educating their children about sex?

Answer   *Jazakum Allah Khayran* for realizing the importance of raising your children based on proper knowledge and also for being aware that, once your children are ready to receive a certain training, you must provide them with such training in the best possible way. This is commendable.

Educating children about sex is a very gradual and long process. It starts from a very young age and takes various paths. It also requires wisdom from the parents in order to prepare the children and put them in the right mind set for when they reach puberty, at which time they will require a more direct approach to sex education.

For children aged two, three and five, sex education will mainly take the form of training to develop the character of *hayaa'* (modesty, healthy balanced shyness, and decency). For Muslims, it is very important to have a character of *hayaa'* to the extent that the Prophet Muhammad *SAAW* said: "For every *deen* there is a core character that distinguishes it, and the core character of Islam is *hayaa'*."[28] Here are some practices that will give you an idea of how to train young children to acquire a character of *hayaa'*:

---

[28] *Al-Isaba*, Version 1.06

• Parents must not let toddlers walk around the house without a diaper. When changing a child's diaper, some parents may unintentionally leave the child without a diaper for some time because they did not have everything ready before starting the process. The child might run around while the parent is busy gathering the rest of the changing gear. Sometimes parents make the mistake of laughing at the child's behaviour, which may look cute. To avoid such a situation, gather everything you need to change the child's diaper and to clean the child before you remove her diaper or underwear. When preparing the child for a bath, do not let her walk around the house naked on her way to the bathroom. If you decide to take off the child's clothes in her room, cover her with a towel and remove the towel in the bathroom.

• When children reach the age of four, parents should start teaching them about the concept of awrah and covering the private parts of the body. Parents should also instruct and train them that when they are using the washroom they should not allow others (friends or anybody) to enter the washroom with them. They should explain to the children that if they need help in the bathroom, only parents or the person looking after them with the permission of their parents can enter the bathroom with them.

• At the age of four, children should also be instructed to knock on the door before entering a room whenever the door is closed. As the children get older, parents need to emphasize this behaviour more.

• Around the age of five or six, children begin to be aware of gender differences. At that age, boys prefer to play with boys and girls prefer to play with girls. This is a suitable time to start teaching children about avoiding close physical contact, such as hugging and kissing, with the other gender. Also at this age, children should start wearing reasonably decent clothing. Skin-tight and very revealing clothing should be avoided for both boys and girls. (We do not mean that girls should be wearing *hijab* at this age).

• Later, when children are around the age of seven, it is always recommended that swimsuits be chosen to promote the character of *hayaa'* in the child. For example, boys should avoid very short or tight swimming trunks. Parents should encourage them to wear loose and long shorts. Girls should be encouraged to wear T-shirts and shorts over their swimsuits.

• In addition to following the above tips, parents must ensure that the family observes Islamic manners in the home environment in terms of the TV programs they watch and the language used by the parents and older siblings. Remember that role modeling is the best method of parenting. .

My son is six years old. He is a nice, well-behaved boy, but sometimes he asks embarrassing questions that I do not know how to handle. Here are a couple of questions he asked lately:

1. Where did I come from?
2. Mom and Dad, do you kiss every night?

Could you please advise me on how to answer these questions to a six year old?

Answer   *Jazak Allah Khayran* for your question. Children start asking questions very early in their lives. Learning to handle these questions properly will prepare parents to educate their children in all life matters. Gender relations and the appropriateness of different acts at different times and in different situations (such as what is appropriate for married people and what is appropriate for unmarried people) is one area where children can learn a lot based on our answers to their questions. Children need to be taught that there is a right time and right conditions for every human action, and if the time and conditions are right, the action is right and beautiful. However, if the time or conditions are not right, the same action can be wrong and ugly.

As parents, we must realize that answering a child's questions is very important for building trust and good communication between us. Reprimanding children for asking questions, or trying to escape from answering them, will send the message that it is wrong to ask questions to their parents, which will push them away and drive them to find answers from other sources. If parents let this happen, they lose a great opportunity to teach their children their values. Parents should always welcome their children's questions and tell their children that they can approach them with any questions or concerns that they have at any time. There is no such thing as embarrassing or inappropriate questions between children and their parents.

Another point for parents to consider is that when a child asks a question, he is ready to hear and learn about the subject matter of the question. By answering the question, parents are teaching their values to a child who is fully attentive and most ready to receive the answer.

Many parents feel awkward and embarrassed about some of their children's questions, which leads them to avoid answering them. As parents, we need to remind ourselves that when a child asks a question he does not know all the facts that the parents know about the subject in question. The child's question is based on certain observations he made in his environment. He is basically trying to make sense of his observations and understand the rules on which they are based. The parents' answer should be true and should only include facts that are appropriate for the child's age and ability to comprehend.

• Let us now take the example of a six year old who asks: "Where did I come from?" This is an opportunity to plant a few concepts in your child's mind, such as:

    – Allah *SWT* is the Creator.

    – A child is a wonderful gift to parents from Allah *SWT*, and the parents must love and care for that gift.

    – *Du'a* is an important part of a Muslim's life. You can ask Allah *SWT* for whatever you want. By making *du'a*, Muslims become closer to Allah *SWT*, who likes us to make *du'a*.

    – Parents must cooperate with each other.

    – Children are given to married people, or marriage is a prerequisite for having children.

The answer to such a question could simply be: "Allah *SWT* created you in Mom's womb. Because Mom and Dad were very happy to get married, we kept praying to Allah *SWT* to bless us with a beautiful child who would make us even happier. Allah *SWT* answered our *du'a* and created you, first as a very tiny baby in Mom's tummy. While you were there, you kept growing and growing until you had two little hands and two little feet, two beautiful eyes, a mouth, and a nose. You had one strong heart and two strong lungs. Then there was no more room for you to grow anymore in Mom's tummy. Allah *SWT* wanted you to have more room to grow and move around, so you could use your two little hands and two little feet, so you could run and clap your hands, and so you could drink milk and say *alhamdulillah*. So Allah *SWT* made you be born, and it was your birthday. At first you cried whenever you got hungry, and your mother fed you only milk. Then you learned to eat and to talk and *masha' a* Allah you are still learning new things every day."

This sort of answer will most likely satisfy the child for some time. The child may ask the same question again. The child might like to hear the answer several times from the parent and think the whole story is fascinating and interesting. Do not be surprised to hear the child repeating the question. Tell him the answer in an interesting story-like format that mentions a lot about the child when he was younger, stressing how dear he is to you.

If the child is searching for a more detailed answer, you will sense it in the way he is asking the question. For example he may say: "But how did it happen?" You can then answer that Allah *SWT* makes the tiny baby come out of the mother's tummy the way a chicken lays an egg. Allah *SWT* is able to make things happen. (It is beneficial to visit a farm and give the child the opportunity to watch animals and their babies. If possible, watch a chicken laying an egg. You can also look for picture storybooks about animals and their youngsters, about how their mothers or parents care for them, and about how young animals learn survival skills gradually.)

• Let us take the example of the second question: "Mom and Dad, do you kiss every night?" Many parents might feel embarrassed by such a question, thinking that the child is asking about sex related kisses, and may even get upset with the child for asking such a question. Because of this, their response may be "Don't ask such a question. That is not polite." What parents must do whenever their child asks a question is to take a moment to think about the question before they even attempt to answer it. When they do this, they will discover that any question is very innocent from the child's perspective. For example, he probably noticed that his mom or dad kisses him goodnight before he goes to bed and never saw his parents kissing each other. Naturally, this makes him wonder whether his parents kiss each other goodnight before going to bed. The answer to this question should simply be: "Yes, dear. Just as Mom and Dad kiss you goodnight, we kiss each other goodnight, too. We are a loving family. Mom and Dad love each other and we love you very much, and we all kiss each other goodnight." Answering the question in this manner will assure the child that the mother and father are on good terms, which will give him a sense of security, in case he may have overheard his parents arguing or disagreeing about something.

Again, we would like to stress that all parents should encourage their children to ask them questions. Parents must do their best to answer their children's questions because it will help build trust and good communication between them.

My daughter is nine years old. Is she old enough for me to talk with her about sex or is she still too young?

Answer Many girls around the age of nine start experiencing some physical changes in their bodies as they approach puberty. The girl herself will be very aware of such changes even though they may not be obvious to others. These physical changes could cause her to feel uncomfortable, confused, and insecure about what is going on with her body. At this stage, girls are likely to become oversensitive and emotional.

The age of puberty varies from one child to another. Therefore, if your nine-year-old daughter is not showing any signs of puberty, it is still a good idea to talk with her about it, since she is probably noticing that her classmates or friends are showing obvious physical changes and may be wondering about the whole matter.

It is advisable that you talk with her and discuss the following:

• Puberty is a stage in which a person goes from being a child to being an adult.

• The age of puberty varies among people, and as long as they are taking care of themselves by eating healthy and sleeping enough hours at night they should not worry about when it happens.

• There are changes associated with puberty. Parents could start by talking about some of the physical changes in one session and by talking more about it in a later session.

• There are responsibilities and obligations that come with being an adult, starting at the age of puberty. Explain that once people become adults they become accountable to Allah *SWT* for their behaviour and actions. That is why it is very important to perform prayers at the right time and correctly observe other acts of worship. It is equally important to treat parents with respect, look after their body and health, take care of their personal responsibilities, such as school, managing their time properly and making the best use of it, select good friends and be in good company, and make good use of the blessings and bounties given to them by Allah *SWT*.

We refer the reader to the next question (Question 44) for more details on how to speak with this age group about this subject. .

*My daughter is 12 years old.
I have noticed some physical
changes happening to her.
I believe in an open relationship between parents and children. However,
I do not know how to approach the matter of sex education and puberty
with her. Please advise me on how to go about this. Thank you.*

Answer An open relationship between parents and children
is an Islamic concept that is highly recommended.
Parents are the keenest and most caring people when it comes to their
children, and it is in the best interest of the youth that they approach their
parents with any questions or concerns they may have. However, most
teens do not do this and shy away from discussing their concerns with
their parents or from asking them questions. One thing that parents can do
to encourage their children to always seek their advice is to listen to them
attentively, empathize, and show care regarding their children's concerns.
Parents can then explain their point of view, clarify the matter, and offer
the best solution.

When talking to teenagers about puberty and the body changes they are
experiencing, parents are advised to do it in a holistic way, so that it is
linked to Islamic values and morals as well as to all the corresponding
responsibilities and duties. We recommend that parents bring the Qur'an
in while addressing this matter and use Qur'anic verses as a basis for the
discussion. They could also use *ahadith* (the sayings of the Prophet
Muhammad *SAAW*) to reinforce certain concepts. A science book with
clear diagrams of internal body organs could also be helpful. Such books

can be obtained from the public library, or parents can simply draw a diagram if they know how to do this. (Avoid showing diagrams of a naked person to show body parts. There is no real need for doing so and it does not reinforce the value of maintaining a high level of modesty).

If parents are already in the habit of reading Qur'an with their children and of explaining to them the general meaning of the verses they read, this practice will come in handy when it is time to discuss puberty. When a child is approaching puberty, the parent should have a private meeting with her in which they read together from the Qur'an a few relevant verses, such as chapter 40, verse 67:

> "It is He Who has created you from dust, then from a drop (of seed), then from a clot; Then he brings you forth as a child, then (ordains) that you reach the age of full strength and afterward that you become old — though some among you die before — and that you reach an appointed term, in order that you may understand."[29]

The parent should then explain the meaning of these verses and use them as an introduction to a conversation about the whole process of development and maturity. The parent should explain how Allah *SWT* created the first human being (Adam *AS*) from dust, and how Allah *SWT* creates every baby in the mothers' womb and makes the baby develop from one stage to another until the baby reaches full term. After this, the baby is born by Allah's will and progresses through life from one stage to the next until she completes her term on earth and returns to her Creator. Thus, all our energy, all our power, and all our senses are from Allah *SWT*, and at the end of our lives we return to Him.

Then the parent should mention that adolescence is one of these stages of development, which prepares humans to move from childhood to

---

[29](Q40, V67)

adulthood. The parent can explain that during adolescence all of the reproductive organs in the body grow at a fast rate under the effect of the hormones produced in the body by the will of Allah *SWT*, the Creator.

You could explain to your daughter that every baby girl is born with two ovaries, which are already full of many follicles that will produce ovum (eggs), and a uterus, which will be the home for her baby in the future *insha'a* Allah. Show her how to make a fist with her hand to see the size of her uterus, which is exactly the same size. Explain that once she reaches puberty Allah *SWT* makes her body produces hormones called estrogen and progesterone. These hormones make her body change and grow a little bit at a time in order for her to mature one day and become ready to be a mother when she gets married. This process of growing includes the following:

• The ovaries produce one ovum (egg) every month.

• The uterus prepares an inner vascular layer of tissue to receive the ovum every month.

• The breasts grow so they can produce milk for a baby to feed on, when your daughter becomes ready to be a mother after she gets married.

• Hair grows in the underarms and pubic area.

• Other changes also happen that make the girl look more like a woman than a child.

Now the little girl has become a woman and she must learn to carry herself like one. *Alhamdulillah* that we have the guidance of the Qur'an and Sunnah to show us how to do this.

The parent will then talk with the youth about how Allah *SWT* blessed her with a healthy and able body, which she must take care of because it is a trust from Allah *SWT*. The parent will also explain that Allah *SWT* has guided us to a lifestyle that will keep us healthy, happy and good by doing only *halaal* actions and staying away from *haraam* actions.

Allah *SWT* told us very clearly that marriage is the only way for a man and woman to have physical relations. Through marriage, a man and a woman can share their lives together, take care of each other, and take care of the children that will come as a result of this marriage. Based on this, any physical relations between a girl and boy during their youth outside marriage is unlawful and is abusive to the bodies that Allah *SWT* has given to them as a trust. Those who do so are disobeying and displeasing Allah *SWT*, the One who created them in the first place and the One who can take all their power away. Such actions are wrong, and those who do it will suffer the consequences in this life as well as in the Hereafter.

With the youth, parents could also read from Surat Al-Araf (chapter 7) verses 8 to 31, explain the general meaning of the verses, emphasize all the principles mentioned in the verses, and relate these principles to the following points:

• Allah *SWT* set very clear limits for us to observe in our interactions with members of the opposite sex.

• Allah *SWT* ordered women to wear *hijab* and always act modestly.

• Allah *SWT* ordered men to act modestly, lower their gaze, dress decently and not look at girls and women as sex objects.

• Allah *SWT* taught both men and women to respect each other and keep their interactions at a decent level.

The parent could say: "You are very likely to come across girls who are dating or talking to their friends about their crushes. These kinds of actions are *haraam* and they displease Allah *SWT*." The parent could also elaborate on the harm the youth could cause to herself or to others. For example, getting pregnant and having babies that do not have a father or mother who is ready to take care of them, hurting their family, interrupting their education, destroying their future, and above all, displeasing Allah *SWT* and losing His blessings.

The parent should explain to her daughter that when she reaches puberty, her uterus will shed its inner layer every month. The mother also needs to teach her daughter proper hygienic practices and the *fiqh* of the monthly period.[30]

We would like to whisper into the ears of every parent that at this stage of life, your daughter desperately needs you. Be close to her and maintain a very good relationship with her. Be considerate of her feelings. Listen to and reason with her. Be assertive, but loving at the same time. Guide and help her to be close to Allah *SWT* because this is the only way she will be strong and able to rise above temptations.[31]

In question number 52 below, you will find further tips for addressing this issue with this age group to ensure the success of this process.

Note: The above discussions should be carried out over several sessions. Parents should use various opportunities and continue to follow up on this topic. Examples of such opportunities are:

* When the youth comes home from school and talks about incidents that took place at school or on her way home.

* When discussing a request from the youth to go out with her friends to a movie or restaurant.

* When discussing whether she should go on a school trip that includes a sleepover away from home.

• When discussing what time she should come home in the evening.

---

[30] See the books entitled *Fiqh us Sunnah* by *Sh. As-Sayyid Sabiq*, particularly the sections on *Ibadat* in general and Purification in particular. Also see *Raising Children in Islam*, volume one, chapter seven, by *Sh. Abdallah Naseh Elwan* and published by *Dar Al-Salam*.

[31] Please refer to chapters one to five of our book entitled *Muslim Teens: Today's Worry, Tomorrow's Hope*

My daughter is 14 years old. Lately she has been oversensitive and often goes to her room and stays there for long hours by herself. I am concerned about her and the changes in her behaviour. Is there anything I can do to help the situation?

Answer   Being oversensitive and staying alone for a long time is normal behaviour for a teenager. During adolescence, many youth become shy and a bit reserved because of all the physical changes they notice happening to their bodies. Parents can help their teens during this sensitive and crucial time by doing the following:

• Giving the teen more room for independence.

• Treating the teen in a way that shows that the parents are considerate of their feelings and look at them as adults.

• Talking to the youth in a way that shows that you, as a parent, care about her.

• Listening to what she has to say, to show that you value her opinion.

• Educating yourself about the youth environment and issues they face at school.[32] Casually open discussion with your teenager about these social issues and challenges in order to make her feel comfortable in talking to you about her feelings and about any difficulties she may be facing. Listen attentively to her and empathize with her situation.

---

[32] See chapters one and two of our book entitled *Muslim Teens: Today's Worry, Tomorrow's Hope.*

• Help her utilize her time and energy in a productive way by assigning her some adult-like responsibilities.

• Educate the youth regarding puberty, the physical and physiological aspects of it, and the responsibilities that come with being an adult.

• Facilitate and give her an opportunity to be in the company of good friends.

• Help your daughter become elevated spiritually. Take all the necessary steps to help her grow spiritually. For example, read the Qur'an with her, pray in *jama'a* together at home (and encourage her to be the *imam*, leading the prayer, once in a while), and take her to the mosque. Give her an opportunity to experience the beautiful feelings of making the early morning or evening *du'a*, at sunrise and sunset, in an outdoor setting, and help her get into the habit of doing it consistently. Organize a youth group where teenagers can learn together about the Prophet *SAAW*, his Companions, and their heroic actions when faced with worldly temptations.

Q.46 - 49

Question 46

I am the mother of a 12-year-old boy. I feel that my son is at a point where he needs to be educated about sex. I have been asking my husband to do this and discuss the issue with my son. My husband feels that there is no need for this and that the children learn about it on their own. He says: "I don't feel comfortable taking to him about this. After all, nobody talked to me about sex when I was his age." Is there any way I can help my husband with this task?

Question 47

I have a 15-year-old daughter and a 13-year-old son. When my daughter was 11, I discussed different issues with her regarding gender relations and sex. As a single mother, I do not know what to do with my son regarding this issue. Could you please advise me?

Question 48

My son is in grade five, and I was shocked to find out that he knows everything about sex. I am worried about him knowing all of this at his young age. Do you have any advice?

Question 49

I am the father of a fifteen-year-old boy and a nine-year-old girl. I think it is a bad idea to discuss sex with my children since it would just open their eyes to something they are too young to know about anyway. My wife disagrees with me and thinks we should discuss this with them. What is your recommendation?

Answer All of the questions listed above have many issues in common. These are:

1. Whether or not to talk to and educate teens and preteens about sex.

2. If a youth already knows about sex, either from friends or from sex education at school, whether it is still important for the parents to discuss it with him.

3. Whether a mother can talk to her son about sex education. This becomes an issue for single mothers or for mothers whose husbands refuse to educate their sons about sex.

4. How to discuss sex with your child.

Regarding the first issue, it is important to state that Islamically, all our actions should be based on knowledge, and should not be simply haphazard behaviours. Also, it is proven from the *Sunnah* of the Prophet Muhammad *SAAW* that he talked to youth and advised them on this matter. For example, the Prophet *SAAW* said, "O Youth, whoever can afford to marry, then get married, and whoever cannot should fast because this will help him to abstain."[33] The Prophet *SAAW* also gave a lot of other advice regarding this matter.

Another important fact to consider is that children nowadays are already very exposed to this subject. Without looking for it or actively trying to find out about it, children hear about sex at school, on the radio and

---

[33] Al Bukhari, Muslim, and others

television, on the front page of magazines and newspapers while standing in the checkout aisle at the supermarket, and in countless other places. On top of this, the information available from all these sources is ethically and morally completely contradictory to the Islamic perspective. This is why it is crucial for parents to discuss sex with their children and not ignore it, naively expecting that the children will not be exposed to it at all.

Of course, as we just discussed, it is very likely that children already have a lot of information about this subject, but they do not know about it from the right perspective. Leaving them with only the information they get from outside sources is very harmful because, without additional guidance, they will take what they learned from outside as the standard. For example, they will see nothing wrong with having a boyfriend or girlfriend, and in fact will think it is the better thing to do. They will not see any problem with watching indecent movies, going to bars or dance clubs, joining sports teams where boys and girls play together and having physical contact, or talking on the phone with youth of the opposite gender.

Parents should talk and discuss the matter of sex with their children. This is how parents can guide and educate their children about the limits and Islamic etiquette and standards for cross-gender interaction.

Next comes the issue of whether a mother can educate her son about sex. Sex education includes several aspects, some of which a mother should discuss with her son, while others that are more specific are better handled by a father or another trusted man.

A mother should be able to discuss morals, ethics and limits regarding interaction with members of the opposite sex. For example, the mother can make it very clear that marriage is the only lawful way for men and women to be in a physical relationship. She can also let her son know that

his relationship with women or girls should be more formal and profes-
sional, as opposed to overly friendly. She could tell him that it is not suitable for boys and girls to go to movies together, out for lunch, to hang out,
or to talk over the phone or Internet. This rule applies for all girls he inter-
acts with, including classmates that he has known for a long time and
grown up with.

With respect to certain specific aspects of sex education, such as physical
development, personal hygiene, and *fiqh,* ideally, the father should be
the one to have this conversation with the son. However, if this is not
possible, the mother could look for a trusted man to talk to her son, such
as an uncle, a close family friend, or a counselor from a youth group. If
no one is available, she could actively research to find good books on the
topic, including science books that discuss development and *fiqh* books
that discuss hygiene and *fiqh* rules. She should give these books to her
son, tell him they have good information for him to read about, and ask
him to read them. She should also ask him to mark any passages that he
does not understand or that he has questions about. She would then need
to research these issues and come back to him with more material to
answer his questions.

Finally, how should parents discuss sex with their children? When talking
to a teenager about puberty and the body changes they are experiencing,
parents are advised to do it in a holistic manner that links it to Islamic values and morals as well as to the corresponding responsibilities and duties.
We recommend that parents bring the Qur'an in when addressing this
matter and use *Qur'anic* verses as a basis for the discussion. They could
also use *ahadith* (the sayings of the Prophet Muhammad *SAAW*) to reinforce certain concepts. A science book with clear diagrams of internal
body organs could also be helpful. Such books can be obtained from the
public library, or parents can simply draw a diagram if they know how to
do this. (Avoid showing diagrams of a naked person to show body parts.
There is no real need for doing so and it does not reinforce the value of
maintaining a high level of modesty).

If parents are already in the habit of reading Qur'an with their children and of explaining to them the general meaning of the verses they read, this practice will come in handy when it is time to discuss puberty. When a child is approaching puberty, the parent should have a private meeting with him in which they read together from the Qur'an a few relevant verses, such as chapter 40, verse 67:

> "It is He Who has created you from dust, then from a drop (of seed), then from a clot; Then he brings you forth as a child, then (ordains) that you reach the age of full strength and afterward that you become old — though some among you die before — and that you reach an appointed term, in order that you may understand."[34]

The parent should then explain the meaning of these verses and use them as an introduction to a conversation about the whole process of development and maturity. The parent should explain how Allah *SWT* created the first human being (Adam *AS*) from dust, and then how Allah *SWT* creates every baby in the mothers' womb and makes the baby develop from one stage to another until the baby reaches full term. After this, the baby is born by Allah's will and progresses through life from one stage to the next until she completes her term on earth and returns to her Creator. Thus, all our energy, all our power, and all our senses are from Allah *SWT*, and at the end of our lives we return to Him *SWT*.

On the Day of Judgment, Allah *SWT* will ask every one of us about how we used our lives and the powers given to us, and He will hold us accountable for what we did. This is why we should always focus on living our lives and doing things the way Allah *SWT* advised us to do them. When others around us are doing wrong and doing *haraam* things, we should not follow them. Instead, we should do the right thing, even if we are the only ones doing so. The Prophet *SAAW* said: "Let no one of you be a blind follower: whenever people do the right thing, he does it.

---

[34] (Q40, V67)

And whenever people do the wrong thing, he does it. Train yourself so that, when people do the right thing, you also do it, and when people do the wrong thing, you abstain from it."[35]

Then the parent should mention that adolescence is one of the stages of development, which prepares humans to move from childhood to adulthood. The parent can explain that during adolescence all of the reproductive organs in the body grow at a fast rate under the effect of the hormones produced in the body by the will of Allah *SWT*, the Creator.

Here, we will discuss how to talk with a teenage boy, since how to talk with a teen girl is covered in a previous question.

Explain to the boy that once he reaches puberty, Allah *SWT* makes his body produce hormones called testosterone and androgens. These hormones make his body change. He may notice the growth of hair on his face, like a beard, and in other parts of his body, such as the pubic area and the underarms. His muscles and bones will get bigger and stronger. His voice will become deeper, like a man's voice. Other changes will also occur, and he will grow a little bit at a time in order to mature one day and become a full grown man who is ready to get married, be a father, take care of his family and look after his wife and children.

Once a boy becomes a man he must learn how to carry himself like one. *Alhamdulillah* that we have the guidance of the Qur'an and Sunnah to show us how to do this. The parent can then talk to the youth about how Allah *SWT* blessed him with a healthy and able body, which he must take care of because it is a trust from Allah *SWT*. The parent can also explain that Allah *SWT* has guided us to a lifestyle that will keep us healthy, happy and good by doing only *halaal* actions and staying away from *haraam* actions.

---

[35] Tirmidhi

In another private session of reading Qur'an with your son, read together from *Surat Al-Araf*, verses 8 to 36. After explaining the general meaning, reflect on and emphasize all the Islamic concepts included in those verses. Continue to explain that during adolescence teenagers feel strong emotions and attraction toward members of the opposite sex, basically because their emotions are still in the process of maturing while their bodies mature at a much faster rate. "It is normal to feel that you have a crush on a girl, but what is important is that you control your feelings and do not act upon them. Though your feelings are very real and over-whelming to you, they will change and go away if you deal with them properly. Allah *SWT* has put a mechanism in your body to help release this energy and these feelings without you having to do anything *haraam*. This happens in the form of what is called a "wet dream" in which your body releases a certain secretion during your sleep. This is usually accompanied by a dream of a more or less romantic nature. This process helps the teenage boy return to a more neutral and calmer emotional state.

"Those who do not control their urges and who act upon their feelings, who start dating or talking to their friends about their crushes are certain-ly doing something *haraam*, which displeases Allah *SWT*." (The parent could elaborate more on the harm that the youth could cause to himself or to others. For example, getting a girl pregnant and having babies that do not have a father or mother who is ready to take care of them, hurting their family, interrupting their education, destroying their future, and above all, displeasing Allah *SWT* and losing His blessings).

The parent could talk about the *hadith* of the Prophet Muhammad *SAAW* that indicates that among the seven categories of people who will be shaded by the mercy of Allah *SWT* on the Day of Judgment is a youth who grows up fulfilling his duties, and obeying and worshipping Allah *SWT*.[36] The parent can explain that Allah *SWT* has given the youth who does these things such a high status because He knows how difficult it is.

---

[36] Al-Bukhari, Muslim, and Al-Nisai

The parent can continue to talk to his son on a more direct and personal level saying something like: "I always pray to Allah *SWT* that He make you one of these youth. I know you can be a right servant to Allah *SWT* and always do only *halaal* actions, and that I will see you in the highest level of *jannah insha'a* Allah. My dear son, stay away from any *haraam* actions even if you see almost everybody else doing them. You will see many boys who have girlfriends hanging out on the streets, going to '*R*' rated movies, and so on. Do not follow them in doing wrong and be among the believers whom Allah *SWT* described as those who are guarding their chastity and constant in their acts of obedience.[37] I assure you that you are not going to be missing out on anything.

"There is a right time and right conditions for everything. Allah told us very clearly that marriage is the only way for a man and woman to have physical relations. Through marriage, a man and woman can share their lives together, enjoy each other, take care of each other, and take care of the children that will come as a result of this marriage. This way, Allah *SWT* will bless you and always be on your side, and you will be in His shade on the Day of Judgment."

We would like to whisper into the ears of every parent that at this stage of life, your son desperately needs you. Be close to him and maintain a very good relationship with him. Be considerate of his feelings. Listen to and reason with him. Be assertive but loving at the same time. Guide him and help him to be close to Allah *SWT* because this is the only way he will be strong and able to rise above temptations.[38]

In question number 52 below, you will find further tips for addressing this issue with this age group, to ensure the success of this process.

---

[37] (Q23, V1-5)

[38] Please refer to chapters one to five of our book entitled *Muslim Teens: Today's Worry, Tomorrow's Hope.*

Note: The above discussions should be carried out over several sessions. Parents should use various opportunities and continue to follow up on this topic. Examples of such opportunities are:

• When the youth comes home from school and talks about incidents that took place at school or on his way home.

• When discussing a request from the youth to go out with his friends to a movie or restaurant.

• When discussing whether he should go on a school trip that includes a sleepover away from home.

• When discussing what time he should come home in the evening.

As you know, sex education is now taught in grade five of elementary school. Is this appropriate for our Muslim child?

Answer Sex education is a part of the curriculum in public schools; however, parents have the right to review the material presented and refuse that their children be taught any aspect of the curriculum that they do not agree with.

In addition, parents must find out in what kind of setting this sex education will take place: whether the class rooms will be co-ed or separate for boys and girls.

If the parents find out that the material being taught is acceptable and that girls and boys are taught separately, they should allow the children to participate in that class. If this is the case, parents also have a duty to follow up at home with discussion about the Islamic perspective on sexuality, connecting it to and emphasizing its moral dimension.

How can I approach the question of dating with my teenage children?

Answer A good method for parents to use with such issues is not to wait until the question is asked or until the subject arises in a conversation. Instead, parents should be proactive. One way of being proactive is to use the opportunity of reciting Qur'an with your children. For example, parents can start a discussion after reading the Qur'an, such as the verses in chapter seven that talk about the creation of Prophet Adam *AS* and the eating from the tree. This is a good opportunity to talk about the relationship between the two genders. It is also a good opportunity to show how Satan whispers and tries to manipulate people into doing wrong.

Then parents can talk to their children in a manner that is suitable for their age, explaining the disadvantages of dating when marriage is not an option and clarifying that there is a right age and a right way to go about the process of marriage.

For any of these pieces of advice to work, it is absolutely crucial for parents to observe the following:

• Parents must have a good, warm, and open relationship with the youth.

• The family atmosphere should be more relaxed.

• Parents should help youth achieve a higher spiritual level and be close to Allah *SWT* by providing them with opportunities to learn and gain Islamic knowledge and to get used to Islamic practices. This could be done by attending youth groups and camps as well as through family learning sessions.

• Parents should help the youth maintain a group of friends who have the same values as you are trying to promote. This way, he has someone he can spend time with, and they can support each other against the negative peer pressure of popular culture.

Ensuring that the above conditions are fulfilled will encourage the youth to ask questions and discuss issues of concern with his parents without hesitation. It will also help children accept their parents' advice because of the strong bond that already exists between them.

I was really shocked and disappointed to discover that my 15-year-old son is going out with a girl at his school. We always tried to raise him to behave as a Muslim should, and he should know that this is wrong. When I asked him why he is doing this, he replied that he loves this girl and cannot live without her. He went on to ask me how this could be wrong when Allah is the One who created these feelings in him.

Answer   This is a very sad situation in which this 15-year-old boy has obviously mistaken a crush for real love.

You need to explain to him that just because humans are created with certain feelings it is not always in their best interest to act upon these feelings. For example, some people have bad tempers, but that does not mean that, when they get angry, they should lash out at people, scream, swear, hit, and do whatever they feel like doing.

As human beings, we are created with the ability to recognize and differentiate good from bad. We are also created with the free will to choose, and are capable of controlling our actions. As humans, we are also occasionally tempted to do wrong.

> "By the soul (Adam or a person or a soul) and Him Who perfected him in proportion; Then He showed him what is wrong for him and what is right for him _ The one who purifies himself is indeed successful, and the one who corrupts himself does indeed fail." [39]

---

[39] (Q91, V7-10)

Temptations are a part of the test of life. Those who understand this, who control their actions and rise above their temptations, are those who will be successful in this life and in the Hereafter. Those who follow their temptations, however, will fail in both worlds. Allah *SWT* created us and He knows what is best for us. .

You should explain to your son that, at the age of 15, a youth is going through the changes caused by puberty, and it is natural for him to have a crush on someone (or on multiple people) and to feel completely consumed by these emotions. Feelings at this stage are very raw, exaggerated and temporary. Thus, it would be a big mistake to build a relationship on these temporary emotions. Those youth who follow their temptations end up harming themselves because these feelings change every few months, and they find themselves constantly "falling in love" with yet another person.

Continue the discussion with your son and explain the example from the *seerah* of the Prophet *SAAW*, which is similar to the case at hand. A young man came to the Prophet *SAAW* and said: "Allow me to fornicate." The Prophet *SAAW* invited the man to come and sit close to him, and he reasoned with him, saying: "Would you like that to happen to your mom? Would you like that to happen to your sister? Would you like that to happen to your aunt?" The young man's answer to each of these questions was: "Of course not, O Prophet of Allah." And the Prophet's reply each time was: "Likewise, other people would not like this to happen to their mothers, sisters, or aunts." After this conversation, the Prophet *SAAW* made *du'a* that Allah *SWT* guide him and make him chaste.[40]

Explaining this to your son is just the first step toward resolving this problem, and it is not enough on its own. Your son needs your support tremendously at this time. The emotions he is experiencing are strong and very real to him.

---

[40] Ahmad

As parents, we can learn a lot from this hadith on how to deal with a young person who has a mistaken idea regarding dating. Some of the lessons we can learn are:

• Parents must reason with and explain to the youth the following:

  – Why its wrong to merely follow and act upon our temptations
  – The consequences of this wrong action on both himself and others
  – How it is not fair to do to others what you would not like to be done to you or someone you love

• Parents must not reject the youth because of his actions. In a case like this, it is natural and instinctive to reject the person. However, unlike his Companions, the Prophet *SAAW* actually brought the person closer to him and sat down with him to talk. Many parents fall into the mistake of allowing their instinctive feelings of anger towards their son take over and dictate how they act with him. This will only cause the situation to worsen, because the more he is rejected by his parents, the more he will feel the need to be in this *haraam* relationship with his "girlfriend" so that he can feel accepted somewhere.

• The parents need to realize that their son is weak and vulnerable, and their focus should be on strengthening him. Some necessary steps to help him through this vulnerable time include:

– Building a strong parent-child bond, especially a father-son bond. This can be done by spending time together. You do not have to only sit and talk. You can play sports together, go grocery shopping or go for a hike or a bike trip (also find out whether your son would like to invite a friend or two along). Give your son more room for independence, and deal with him in a manner that shows you care about him.

– The parents (especially the father) should treat their son in a way that makes him feel valued. For example, take his opinion regarding some family decisions that have to be made and so on.

– Help the son become elevated spiritually. Note that the Prophet *SAAW* made du'a for the boy after reasoning with him. Parents should make sincere *du'a* for their son and teach him to make *du'a* for himself. They should take all the necessary steps to help their son grow spiritually. For example, they should read Qur'an with him, pray in *jama'a* together at home (and ask him to be the *imam*, leading the prayer, once in a while), and take him to the mosque. Also give him an opportunity to experience the beautiful feelings of making the early morning or evening *du'a*, at sunrise and sunset, in an outdoor setting, and help him to get into the habit of doing this consistently. Organize a youth group where they can learn together about the Prophet *SAAW* and his Companions and their heroic actions when facing worldly temptations.

– Search together for healthy and acceptable activities that will consume some of your son's time and energy and fill the emotional gap he is feeling. Sports, youth groups, work, and volunteering activities that contribute to society such as at hospitals, community centres, mosques and Islamic centers are all suggestions.

– The parents should educate the youth about the Islamic perspective on gender relations and clarify that marriage is the only *halaal* and lawful way for a physical relationship to exist between men and women. As the Prophet *SAAW* said: "O youth, whoever can afford to marry, then get married, and whoever cannot should fast because this will help him to abstain."[41]

Finally, we would like to whisper into the ears of every parent that your son desperately needs you to be close and considerate to him and to maintain a good relationship with him. Listen to him and reason with him. Be assertive but loving at the same time. Guide him and help him to be close to Allah *SWT* because this is the only way he will be strong and able to rise above temptations.

---

[41] Al-Bukhari, Muslim, and others

How can parents educate their children about sex in an Islamic manner?

Answer Please refer to the previous questions in this section. In addition, we would like to take the opportunity of this question to emphasize a few important guidelines for parents to consider. These are:

• We should always remind ourselves that the Qur'an talks about matters regarding sex and it is done in the most dignified way. We should try our best to learn from the language and methodology of the Qur'an.

• Parents should not shy away from discussing this subject with their children. The beloved 'A'isha , the Mother of the Faithful *RAA*, complimented the women of the *ansar* for not shying away from asking questions about sex in order to have a good and sound understanding of the affairs of their *deen*.[42] It was said that modesty (*hayaa'*) should not prevent a Muslim from asking or answering questions that are relevant to helping the person have a better understanding of the *deen*.

• Sex is part of life, and we must deal with the issues surrounding it. We should not view it as something dirty as long as it is practiced within the limits and etiquette of Islamic marriage.

• We should always encourage our children to approach us, their parents, with any of their questions or concerns, no matter how young or old the child may be or how difficult and confusing the question is. It is our duty

---

[42] Tahtheeb Sunnan Abu Dawoud

to listen to and properly deal with our children's questions and concerns. When we do not know the answers, it is also our duty to find out.

• We also advise parents to adopt a policy of having an open relationship with their children and of not being critical or judgmental when they ask questions or want to discuss any issue. Parents should try their best to be approachable and friendly.[43] Having a judgmental and critical attitude may turn children away from directing questions to their parents. Because of such an attitude, children may prefer to ask one of their peers or school counselors, who may give them advice that the parents would not like because it goes against their values.

• Sex education is a continuous process, and it is our duty to use various opportunities to provide our children with the proper knowledge about sex that is suitable for their age.

• Our answers to our children's questions about sex should convey only true facts and information, should be appropriate to their age, and should be given using the proper language.

• Make sure that the information you provide is correct and clear. Consult references on the subject if you do not have the proper information yourself.

• Educate yourself about the nature of teenagers and the environment they live in as well as the changes they go through during these years. Gain knowledge about their physical, psychological, spiritual and emotional changes.[44] This will help you to be considerate and understanding of the struggle they are experiencing.

---

[43] Refer to chapters one and three of our book entitled *Muslim Teens: Today's Worry, Tomorrow's Hope*, published by Amana Publications, for tips on how to improve your relationship with your child and be approachable parents.
[44] Same reference as above.

Celebrations

How can we prepare our children for Ramadan even though they are surrounded by a non-Islamic environment at school?

Answer   To prepare children for Ramadan, start one month ahead, or whatever time is left before *Ramadan*, by talking to the children about how excited you are for *Ramadan* to be coming soon *insha'a* Allah. According to the children's age, explain to them why *Ramadan* is so beautiful and good for us, that *Ramadan* is the time for our sins to be forgiven and for rewards to be earned, and that it is an opportunity to do good deeds more easily.

If the children are young, read some Islamic books to them about *Ramadan*. There are many such books available.

If the children are older, read with them the various *ahadith* and verses from the Qur'an that talk about the benefits and special privileges given to us during *Ramadan*.

Make some plans with your children of things they would like to do during *Ramadan*, such as visiting or hosting some of their friends' families, going to a community *iftar*, or going to the mosque on the weekends to pray *taraweeh*.

Talk with them about any special food or desserts they would like you to prepare during *Ramadan*, or some special family time that you could have during *Ramadan*. If the children are young, play games with them that celebrate *Ramadan*, and sing songs with them about *Ramadan*. Prepare some artwork at home with them about *Ramadan*, decorate the house and the rooms with their artwork and make it very obvious all through the house that it is a special time.

Even young children can participate in fasting. Parents can ask them if they would like to fast after breakfast for a couple of hours, or until lunch or dinner time, depending on the child's age. Then, parents can make a big deal of it, being very encouraging of the children and telling everybody in the family that they fasted for a certain period of time. Parents can tell them that they are good Muslims, that Allah *SWT* has given them a lot of reward, and that it has been written for them in their book of good deeds.

When parents practice the Sunnah of the Prophet *SAAW* by fasting voluntarily on Mondays and Thursdays or at other recommended times during the year, this gives them an opportunity to talk about fasting in general, because the children will ask them why they are fasting on these days. It also gives parents an opportunity to remind them of *Ramadan*.

We live in North America. This culture is completely different from Islamic culture. For example, people here celebrate several holidays, such as Halloween at the end of October, Thanksgiving towards the end of November, Christmas towards the end of December, New Year's Day and Valentine's Day. Should we allow our children to participate in these celebrations? If the answer is no, what should we do to prevent our children from feeling inferior to their peers because they do not participate in these celebrations?

Answer This is a very important question that is being asked in almost every workshop we conduct and every lecture we deliver during national conventions and regional conferences in North America. We also receive similar questions via e-mail from Muslims in various parts of the world.

To answer this question we should emphasize the following points:

• As Muslims we must be careful not to group all celebrations into one category. Parents should look at each celebration separately and objectively, and then make an informed decision. For example, Thanksgiving is completely different from Christmas or Halloween.

• Parents should ask themselves the following questions about the celebration under consideration:

  – What is the origin of the celebration?
  – Does it have a religious dimension or connotation?
  – What kind of message will this celebration send to my child?

– What kind of impression is this celebration going
  to have on my child?
– Is it a once-in-a-lifetime event or a regular celebration that
  will be a part of my child's life and personality in the future?

If we ask ourselves these questions about the above-mentioned celebrations, we can easily say that we should not celebrate or allow our children to celebrate Halloween, Christmas, or Valentine's Day.

Thanksgiving, however, may be different. We should give thanks to Allah *SWT* and teach our children to be grateful to Him for all His bounties all the time, not just one day a year. However, if somebody observes Thanksgiving, this is not a sin or a crime.

Having said this, what should parents do at the time of these celebrations, particularly if their children attend public school where these holidays are regularly observed and encouraged by the school system? Here is some advice for every Muslim parent to help them deal with this dilemma:

• Meet your child's teacher early in the school year to tell him or her that your child is a Muslim and will not be celebrating Christmas. However, you do not want your child to miss out on the academic lessons. Since most public school systems use thematic methods for teaching, talking about Christmas in the classroom can start as early as mid-November. Ask the teacher to allow your child to do other activities that are not related to the holiday. For example, your child could draw a star or a crescent instead of a Christmas tree, or write a letter to his grandpa instead of to Santa. This way the child will still be part of the lesson, but with a reduction of the religious aspect of the holiday and its effect on your child.

• On the day of the big Christmas party, do not send your child to school. Make that day special and fun for your child at home. You could invite some of her Muslim friends, who are also not going to school that day, and have a small gathering for them. In addition to the fun time, you can take the opportunity to teach them about Prophet Issa *SAAW*, his miraculous birth, the miracles he performed by Allah's permission, and so on.

• Be careful not to ridicule the holidays and celebrations of others. Some parents may become frustrated and overwhelmed with their children's attraction to the beautiful Christmas decorations, and might make comments such as "Christmas lights are ugly!" This is not right, nor is it true. In addition, it could give your child the wrong impression. In such a situation, parents must always acknowledge that the decoration is nice, that the lights look good, and always tell the truth.

• It is very important to make *Ramadan* and the two *Eid* celebrations very special and filled with fun and good memories for your children, to compensate for them not being a part of the other celebrations.

• Some of the early scholars issued *fatwas* indicating that Muslims should not congratulate non-Muslims on their religious celebrations. These *fatwas* may have been applicable during their time and in their environment, but they are not applicable nowadays or in the North American environment. As a matter of fact, other *fatwas* indicate that there is nothing wrong with extending congratulatory wishes to non-Muslims during their religious celebrations.[45]

Please refer to chapter nine of our book entitled *Muslim Teens: Today's Worry, Tomorrow's Hope* for more tips on how to deal with Christmas and Halloween celebrations. Another good source is the SoundVision Website, where you can find samples of letters to send to your child's school administration to help you say no to such celebrations.[46]

[45] Dr. Yusuf Al-Qaradawy. Contemporary Fatwas Volume 3, Dar Al Qalam for Distribution and Publications, Kuwait, 2001.
[46] SoundVision.com newsletters

Sometimes I find myself in a situation where I do not know how to answer my daughter's questions. She is four years old. She always compares herself to other Muslim children from families we know in the community. How should I answer when she asks me, "How come I can't go trick-or-treating when Mona can?" or "Why can't I go to school for the Christmas party when Zaynab can?"

Answer   Please refer to the previous question, which is related to allowing or not allowing our children to participate in certain activities, such as trick-or-treating, and celebrations, such as Christmas.

As for what you should say to your daughter when she compares herself with other Muslim girls in the community who may be participating in some of these celebrations, we suggest the following:

• Always welcome your child's question and keep a smiling face. Never show disappointment when your child asks you a question, even if you do not know how to answer it. As a matter of fact, parents should always encourage their children to ask questions. It gives the parents an opportunity to discuss and teach their child proper behaviour and moral values. Every question that a child asks may represent a challenge to the parent, but it is also the perfect occasion for parents to interact with the child and give her the proper answer according to her age.

• Empathize with your daughter. Try to put yourself in her position. Tell her that you know how she feels. This will comfort her a lot.

• At the same time, explain to her in a very simple way that we are all going to meet Allah *SWT* on the Day of Judgment as individuals, and we will be judged as individuals. It is not a valid excuse for any one of us to say "But so-and-so was doing the same thing." You may also read for her the verse in *Surat Maryam*, which says: "And every one of them will appear before Allah on Resurrection day in a lonely state."[47] You can also recite the verse of *Surat Al-Ana' am* that says: "And now indeed you have come to Us in a lonely state, even as We created you in the first instance."[48]

• It may also be a good idea to tell your daughter that people are different. All Muslims try their best to obey Allah *SWT*. Some may be able to obey most of Allah's orders, and others may be able to obey only some of them.We should always try to apply all of Allah's orders, and when we see somebody who is not applying them, we should try to remind her and help her in a nice and kind way, rather than imitate her and do what she is doing.

---

[47] (Q19, V95)
[48] (Q6, V94)

My daughter is 16 years old. She has been attending public school. She is graduating from high school this year insha'a Allah. It is early, but I am expecting her to ask me about going to the prom. I feel that it is not proper for a Muslim girl to attend such a party and I have been hinting to this, but we never discuss it in detail with her (neither myself, nor her father). I am very concerned about this and do not know how to discuss it with her. Can you please advise me on the best way to go about this? Jazakum Allah Khayran.

Answer This is a very important question that usually occupies the minds of many parents. Prom is an unacceptable activity for Muslims. It includes dancing and drinking. It is also held in an environment of free mixing between boys and girls. All these factors make it an unacceptable activity for a Muslim to attend.

The question now is how to make sure that our teenagers understand this and that they are willing to endure not being a part of the group during this final gathering with their peers to bring closure to an important stage of their life.

As a parent, you can do this by talking to your daughter in a kind manner, recognizing and legitimizing her wish to go and see her friends, say goodbye, attend this celebration, and be a part of everybody's last memory. Tell her that you really understand her feelings and know that it would mean a lot to her to attend. Show her that you recognize how sad it is for her not to be able to participate. Tell her, however, that it is too bad that prom includes dancing, drinking and free mixing between members of the opposite sex, because that makes it impossible for her to participate in it.

Although she cannot participate in prom, she still needs to say goodbye to her friends in a *halaal* way that will also be a good memory for her. Together with your daughter, you should brainstorm ways of doing this, taking into consideration that it should be girls only and should not include Islamically objectionable things. Some examples could be:

• Having a party at your home hosted by your daughter for her girlfriends

• Going together to a restaurant for lunch and spending the afternoon in a park

• Going together to a bowling alley for few games and then having dinner together in your home

We hope this will help you with your daughter. Be kind and gentle when you talk to her. We make *du'a* to Allah *SWT* for your success.

My husband and I are always arguing about celebrating our child's birthday. He says there is nothing wrong with it, while I think birthdays should not be celebrated. After all, wouldn't celebrating birthdays be a blind imitation of a Western tradition? Can you please tell us whether or not it is proper to celebrate birthdays? Jazakum Allah Khayran.

Answer To answer this question properly we have to keep in mind four basic Islamic principles. These are:

1. **The basic *asl*[49] refers to the permissibility of things.** This principle, established by Islam, denotes that things that Allah *SWT* has created and the benefits derived from them are essentially for man's use, and are therefore permissible. Nothing is *haraam* except what is prohibited by a sound and explicit text from the Lawgiver, Allah *SWT*. If the text is not sound, as in the case of a weak *hadith*, or if it is not explicit in stating the prohibition, the original principle of permissibility applies.

2. "When the Prophet *SAAW* came to Madinah, he found that they had two days of celebration and feasts. He told them that **Allah *SWT* has replaced these two days with two better days**: the two *Eids, Eid ul Adha* and *Eid ul Fitr*."[50] It is clear from this hadith that the Prophet *SAAW* limited annual celebrations to only the two *Eids*.

---

[49] *Asl*, plural usul, denotes origin, source, foundation, basis, fundamental or principle.
[50] Muslim

3. **"Every soul is responsible for what it earns."**[51] The concept of accountability is deeply entrenched in the Islamic system, in all areas and at all levels. Muslims are always encouraged to look deeply into the expected consequences of any action before doing it. If the consequences are expected to cause definite harm, Muslims should try to avoid the action. If the consequences are expected to bring benefits, it is good to do such an action.

4. **Choose the lesser of two evils.** This is a great rule in Islamic jurisprudence that was deduced by the scholars from the practices of the Prophet *SAAW* and the teachings of Qur'an. This rule should be understood properly and applied wisely by parents in the North American environment.

Based on the first principle, some say that there is nothing wrong with celebrating birthdays, since there is no specific text prohibiting it. However, looking at the second principle, we see that the Prophet *SAAW* clearly instructed us that nothing should be celebrated annually or observed regularly except the two *Eids*: *Al Fitr* and *Al Adha*. Also, the fact that the practice of celebrating birthdays was not known among the early Muslims may raise the question "Why should we start promoting a Western tradition that may not be proper?"

Bearing in mind the above arguments so far, the least that could be said about celebrating birthdays is that it is a questionable or controversial practice. However, this is not the end of the story. There are other factors that should be considered in the North American environment, such as the consequences of celebrating versus ignoring birthdays.

Among the unacceptable consequences of celebrating birthdays in the current Western format is that the birthday person is the centre of attention and the only person who feels special during the celebration. This may promote traces of arrogance in the personality of some children and make them full of themselves. Also, the celebration format may be unacceptable to some because of the lavish gifts that some parents buy for their children and the time wasted just eating and playing games.

---

[51](Q74, V38)

On the other hand, ignoring the birthday of a school-age child may lead the child to think that his parents do not care about him and that his teacher loves him much more than his parents. This is because teachers in public schools usually wish the children a happy birthday and may even have a little celebration in the class. We do not think that any parent would like to leave his or her child with such an impression.

Clearly, the answer to this question is not a simple yes or no. All of the above factors must be taken into consideration, and the answer could vary from one situation to another, depending on the child's age and specific conditions.

The reality is that most Muslim parents now in North America celebrate their children's birthdays. Our objective should be for our Muslim children to give up these celebrations in their current format. However, this objective, though noble, cannot be achieved in only one step. With the parents' wisdom in dealing with the situation *insha'a* Allah this objective can be achieved gradually. Here is what we suggest to achieve this goal *insha'a* Allah in the most amicable way while avoiding the negative consequences discussed earlier:

• When the child is very young (one to four years old) and is not yet attending school, there is no need for the parents to initiate a birthday celebration for her. No harmful effects can be expected from this practice, because the child is not likely to notice that other children are celebrating their birthdays.

• If the child is school age, it would be a big mistake to completely ignore the issue of birthdays. In such a situation, the answer could be to celebrate the child's birthday but in a manner that is low-key. For example, the child could invite two or three of his friends, have a cake and some food that he likes, and play a few games with his friends. He could sit with his parents, either before his friends arrive or after they leave, and discuss what he wants to do throughout the coming year to learn more and be a better person. Thus, you shift the focus of the celebration away from the food and games toward a more Islamic format of self-evaluation for improvement. This way, as the child is being entertained, he is also learning an important Islamic concept: the concept of self-assessment and auditing our deeds (*muhassabah*). Parents could use the opportunity to congratulate him for his achievements in the past year. They could also remind him that birthdays are not really big celebrations in Islam, but that they are celebrating his birthday now so he does not feel left out or feel bad. Parents could mention the *hadith* of the Prophet *SAAW* that Allah *SWT* has replaced all celebrations with two meaningful celebrations: *Eid ul Fitr* and *Eid ul Adha*. This way you have chosen the lesser harm (of having a limited and small-scale celebration in an acceptable format) to avoid a greater harm (the child's feeling that his parents do not love him and that his school teacher loves him more). Tell the child that, once he is ready to let go of celebrating his birthday, he should tell you. By then you would be fully applying the *hadith* of the Prophet *SAAW*.

In addition to the above gradual approach to help your child give up celebrating birthdays, always make the celebrations of the two *Eids* much bigger and more entertaining for him in every aspect: in the home environment, and with gifts and new clothes so that he can enjoy it more than any birthday.

Another suggestion is that you explain to the children that, during *Eid*, all Muslims are happy and feel special, while at a birthday party only one person feels special.

Miscellaneous

What could cause a child to be hyperactive? I think that my five-year-old boy is very hyperactive because he jumps a lot on the bed and keeps running around the apartment, which makes noise and disturbs the neighbors. What can I do, observe, or look for to avoid or minimize his hyperactive behaviour?

Answer Children are full of energy, which they must channel in the proper direction. They need to run around, play ball and jump regularly to get rid of this energy. Current lifestyles do not usually give children an opportunity to do this, especially if they are living in an apartment building. Parents should make sure that their children are given the opportunity to go out to the park often enough to get rid of any excess energy they may have. If parents cannot take the child regularly to the playground or park, they should modify their living quarters to suit the child's need for activity. For example, if you live in a three-bedroom apartment, designate one room for the children to use as a playroom. In this room, parents should spread a couple of mattresses on the floor to allow the children to jump without disturbing the neighbors. Even with a playroom, parents should still give children the opportunity to occasionally go out.

Here are some things that you should be monitoring to prevent your children from becoming hyperactive:

• Watch what kind of food they eat and what kind of diet they are following. Are they eating many foods that contain high levels of sugar, preservatives, food colours, and so on? The fluids they drink also have to be observed. How many cans of pop or juice drinks do they have a day? Any foods or drinks that contain high levels of sugar should be consumed in moderation.

• Look at how they spend their time. Do we get them involved in enough structured activities to help them channel their energy in the proper direction and help them in a healthy and positive way? How many times do we take them out for camping, hiking, and sports, for example?

• Check your reaction to the things they do. They may have learned from previous behaviour that the way to get your attention is by being hyperactive. In the past, you may have reacted in a way that perpetuated this pattern of behaviour. If this is so, you have to start changing how you react to their level of activity to make sure it is at a moderate and acceptable level.

How can we encourage
our children to build the
good habit of reading
books? What is our responsibility towards the material they read, and
how can we help them pick the right books that are not harmful to them?

Answer Getting into the habit of reading is very   important.
The first word revealed in Qur'an was *iqra*, which
means *read* or *recite*. Reading is the most important tool for acquiring
knowledge. As Muslims, we are encouraged to continuously seek
knowledge throughout the various stages of our lives.

To help our children acquire good reading habits, we should start very
early with them. When they are young and unable to read by themselves,
we should read to them. We should select nice and interesting stories that
suit their age. We should also make reading to them a fun and loving
experience. Always provide a warm and cozy atmosphere when you
are reading to them. Be animated and excited by acting out the various
characters in the story to keep them interested and make them love the
experience of reading.

Let them read to you when they grow a little older and are able to read
with difficulty. Again, the time you spend together should be fun. Make
sure that the books you select are suitable for their age in terms of the size
of the letters and the story line. Islamic literature is full of wonderful
books with stories about the prophets as well as great Islamic personalities in the history of Islam.

In addition to Islamic books, parents could use many books available at their local public library. However, parents should check to make sure that these books are conveying the proper message   for your child's age.

There is no doubt that we, as parents, are responsible for the material we expose our children to. The Qur'an tells us that we are responsible for what we hear, what we see, and even what goes through our hearts and minds.[52] As such, we should be very careful about which books we read to our children when they are young, and which books we allow them to read when they are older.

---

[52] (Q17, V37)

Is there any relationship between food and children's behavior? If so, could you explain it?

Answer Yes, there is a relationship between the food a child eats and her behavior. The number of children who are allergic to many artificial foods, such as food colouring, preservatives, and refined foods including sugar and white flour is on the rise. Some of these children become hyperactive and have difficulty concentrating. Therefore, we advise parents to feed their children healthy and wholesome food. Get them used to drinking water, which can give them a healthy urinary system. Limit their intake of soft drinks and sweetened juices because the sugar gives them a feeling of fullness and energy, making them think that they do not need to eat. In addition, the carbonation in soft drinks prevents calcium from building up in their bones, leading to weaker bones. On top of all this, the sugar level in their blood oscillates after drinking these sweetened drinks, which causes them to be restless, hyperactive and unable to concentrate. Children should eat fresh vegetables and fruits, whole grain wheat and rice, honey and molasses (which are better than jam or chocolate), and peanut butter.

I have a 19-year-old daughter, who is a university student. Just a few days ago she told me that there is a boy in her class who wants to marry her. She says that she trusts him enough and thinks that she would be able to live happily with him. She said that she is ready to accept whatever my decision is. She has been saying no to this boy for a long time because she thought that I would feel very bad if she said yes to him. She says she will never do anything that I am not ready to approve. What should I do?

Answer   Firstly, we would like to commend you for having such a strong bond with your daughter, to the extent that she wants your approval for her marriage.

Secondly, we assume that the boy she would like to marry is a Muslim. In this case, talk with your daughter about what she is looking for in the man she would like to marry, perhaps even going as far as writing down a list of qualities. Discuss what she wants her family life to be like after marriage. Through this discussion, you can guide your daughter to have a clear idea about the attributes of a good husband and how they are going to affect her quality of life. Examples of attributes to look for in a husband are: whether he observes his prayers, whether he is polite and good tempered, and whether he lives and judges things in accordance with the rulings of Islam.

If the boy does have a good character, then you should look deeper into the issue because he may be a good match for your daughter. However, you must pay some attention to his ability to support himself and his wife.

We do not mean that you should be materialistic, but rather that you should think realistically about marriage responsibilities.

Consider the boy's age in terms of his suitability for being responsible for your daughter. If he is as young as your daughter, make sure that you are sure about his level of maturity and responsibility for marriage.

One more important piece of advice is that you should fully involve the boy's family in the marriage process and make sure that his family is fully aware of it. For further details on how to go about the process of a proper marriage, please consult chapter three of our new book entitled *Blissful Marriage: A Practical Islamic Guide,* published by Amana Publications.

References

———. *The Noble Qur'an, English Translation of the Meanings and Commentary*. Medina, Kingdom of Saudi Arabia: King Fahd Complex for the Printing of the Holy Qur'an, 1417 A.H.

Beshir, Dr. Ekram and Mohamed Rida Beshir. *Meeting the Challenge of Parenting in the West, An Islamic Perspective*, second edition. Beltsville, Maryland: Amana Publications, 2000.

Beshir, Dr. Ekram and Mohamed Rida Beshir. *Muslim Teens: Today's Worry, Tomorrow's Hope*, first edition. Beltsville, Maryland: Amana Publications, 2001.

Imam Abi Al-Husain Muslim Ibn Al-Haggag Al-Qushairee Al-Naisabouree. *Sahih Muslim,* first edition. Cairo: *Dar Ihiaa' Alkutob Alarabia*, 1955.

Imam Abi Abdellah Muhammad Ibn Ismail Ibn Ibraheem Ibn Al-Mogheirah Ibn Bardezabah Al-Bukhari. *Sahih al-Bukhari*, Cairo, *Dar Al Shaa'b.*

Imam Al-Hafez Abi Dawud Sulaiman Ibn Al-Asha'th Al-Sagestany Al-Azdei. *Sunan Aby Dawud,* first edition. Beirut, *Dar Ibn Hazm*, 1998.

Imam Al-Hafez Aby Abderahaman Ahmad Ibn Shua'ib Ibn Ali Ibn Senan Ibn Dinar Al-Nisa'i. *Sunan Al-Nisa'i,* first edition. Beirut, *Dar Ibn Hazm,* 1999.

Imam Ibn Majah. *Sunan Ibn Majah*, first edition. Cairo, *Dar Ihiaa'At Turath Al-A'raby*, 1975.

Imam Malik Ibn Anas. Mowata' *Al Imam Malek*, ninth edition. Beirut, *Dar Al-Nafae's,* 1985. Prepared by Ahmad Rateb Armoosh.

Other books of Hadith, *Ahmad, Tabarani, Tirmidhi,* and so on.

Gawad, Mohammad., *Al-Imam Ali encyclopedia,* volume one. *Dar Al-Tayar Al-Jadded.*

Spock, Benjamin. *Dr. Spock's Baby and Child Care* eighth edition. New York: Pocket Books.

Al-Ghazaly, Shaykh Muhammad, *Muslim Character*, first edition. Salimiah, Kuwait: International Islamic Federation of Student Organizations, 1983.

Shaykh Abdul Fattah Abu Ghudda, *Islamic manners*. Swansea, U.K.: Awakening Publications, 2001.